TV SPORT STARS OF
FORMULA ONE
ANNUAL 2014

Written by Jon Culley

Designed by Lucy Boyd

A Pillar Box Red Publication

© 2013. Published by Pillar Box Red Publishing Ltd.

ISBN 978-1-907823-69-5

Images © Action Images.com

Contents

Sebastian Vettel

How to stop Sebastian Vettel? A problem to which so far the rest of the field in Formula One have struggled to find the answer since the German won his maiden world championship in 2010.

The Red Bull driver has simply dominated in recent years, usurping the 2009 winner Lewis Hamilton as the youngest drivers' champion in history at the age of 23.

In 2011, Vettel secured a second successive drivers' championship, amassing a mammoth 392 points after nabbing an incredible 11 race wins, 15 poles and 17 podiums in the 19-race season. That astounding return was unsurprisingly a Formula One record, although setting precedents has proved a habit for Vettel.

His other records include being the youngest driver and youngest points scorer – both achieved aged 19 – and

the youngest race winner after his maiden triumph at the 2008 Italian Grand Prix while driving for Toro Rosso.

Two years ago, he became the youngest triple world champion, beating Ayrton Senna's previous record by an astonishing six years. His 2012 success was closer – Ferrari's Fernando Alonso working a minor miracle to push him all the way – but he ultimately prevailed by just three points after his Spanish rival failed to win the final race in Brazil.

Vettel's unwavering competitiveness and ruthless determination has sometimes been the subject of

criticism, as suggested by his periodic disagreements with former teammate Mark Webber, although the self-confessed anglophile is known – like previous greats such as Senna and Michael Schumacher – for his sense of humour and easy-going personality away from the track.

Vettel first attracted serious attention in the German BMW ADAC series, finishing 2nd in 2003 and dominating in 2004, when he was champion with a staggering 18 wins from 20 races.

In 2005 he stepped up to F3 Euro Series, finishing 5th behind Lewis Hamilton and runner-up to another Brit, Paul di Resta, in 2006.

He was afforded his F1 break at the US Grand Prix in Indianapolis the same year when he replaced the injured BMW Sauber driver Robert Kubica and finished 8th.

The switch to Toro Rosso raised his standing still further and Red Bull recruited him for the 2009 season, in which he only narrowly lost to McLaren's Jenson Button in a thrilling title race.

The progression to world champion was inevitable, although his maiden crown in 2010 was not secured until the last race in Abu Dhabi, where he overtook Alonso and Webber in the standings by winning the Grand Prix from pole.

FACT PANEL

BORN: July 3, 1987; Heppenheim, West Germany
2013 TEAM: Red Bull
DEBUT: 2007 United States GP (BMW Sauber)
FIRST F1 WIN: 2008 Italian GP (Toro Rosso)
FIRST F1 TITLE: 2010 (Red Bull)

World Champion Drivers – 1950-2012

Year	Driver	Constructor
1950	Giuseppe Farina (Italy)	Alfa Romeo
1951	Juan Manuel Fangio (Argentina)	Alfa Romeo
1952	Alberto Ascari (Italy)	Ferrari
1953	Alberto Ascari (Italy)	Ferrari
1954	Juan Manuel Fangio (Argentina)	Maserati Mercedes
1955	Juan Manuel Fangio (Argentina)	Mercedes
1956	Juan Manuel Fangio (Argentina)	Ferrari
1957	Juan Manuel Fangio (Argentina)	Maserati
1958	Mike Hawthorn (Great Britain)	Ferrari
1959	Jack Brabham (Australia)	Cooper
1960	Jack Brabham (Australia)	Cooper
1961	Phil Hill (United States)	Ferrari
1962	Graham Hill (Great Britain)	BRM
1963	Jim Clark (Great Britain)	Lotus
1964	John Surtees (Great Britain)	Ferrari
1965	Jim Clark (Great Britain)	Lotus
1966	Jack Brabham (Australia)	Brabham
1967	Denny Hulme (New Zealand)	Brabham
1968	Graham Hill (Great Britain)	Lotus
1969	Jackie Stewart (Great Britain)	Matra
1970	Jochen Rindt (Austria)	Lotus
1971	Jackie Stewart (Great Britain)	Tyrell
1972	Emerson Fittipaldi (Brazil)	Lotus
1973	Jackie Stewart (Great Britain)	Tyrell
1974	Emerson Fittipaldi (Brazil)	McLaren
1975	Niki Lauda (Austria)	Ferrari
1976	James Hunt (Great Britain)	McLaren
1977	Niki Lauda (Austria)	Ferrari
1978	Mario Andretti (United States)	Lotus
1979	Jody Scheckter (South Africa)	Ferrari
1980	Alan Jones (Australia)	Williams
1981	Nelson Piquet (Brazil)	Brabham
1982	Keke Rosberg (Finland)	Williams
1983	Nelson Piquet (Brazil)	Brabham
1984	Niki Lauda (Austria)	McLaren
1985	Alain Prost (France)	McLaren
1986	Alain Prost (France)	McLaren
1987	Nelson Piquet (Brazil)	Williams
1988	Ayrton Senna (Brazil)	McLaren
1989	Alain Prost (France)	McLaren
1990	Ayrton Senna (Brazil)	McLaren
1991	Ayrton Senna (Brazil)	McLaren
1992	Nigel Mansell (Great Britain)	Williams
1993	Alain Prost (France)	Williams
1994	Michael Schumacher (Germany)	Benetton
1995	Michael Schumacher (Germany)	Benetton
1996	Damon Hill (Great Britain)	Williams
1997	Jacques Villeneuve (Canada)	Williams
1998	Mika Hakkinen (Finland)	McLaren
1999	Mika Hakkinen (Finland)	McLaren
2000	Michael Schumacher (Germany)	Ferrari
2001	Michael Schumacher (Germany)	Ferrari
2002	Michael Schumacher (Germany)	Ferrari
2003	Michael Schumacher (Germany)	Ferrari
2004	Michael Schumacher (Germany)	Ferrari
2005	Fernando Alonso (Spain)	Renault
2006	Fernando Alonso (Spain)	Renault
2007	Kimi Raikkonen (Finland)	Ferrari
2008	Lewis Hamilton (Great Britain)	McLaren
2009	Jenson Button (Great Britain)	Brawn
2010	Sebastian Vettel (Germany)	Red Bull
2011	Sebastian Vettel (Germany)	Red Bull
2012	Sebastian Vettel (Germany)	Red Bull

MULTIPLE WINNERS

- 7 Michael Schumacher (Germany)
- 5 Juan Manuel Fangio (Argentina)
- 4 Alain Prost (France)

WINNERS BY COUNTRY

- 14 Great Britain
- 10 Germany
- 8 Brazil

WINNERS BY CONSTRUCTOR

15 Ferrari
12 McLaren
7 Williams

MOST GPS CONTESTED

Rubens Barrichello (Brazil) – 322

MOST GPS WON

Michael Schumacher (Germany) – 91

YOUNGEST STARTER

Jaime Alguersuari (Spain) – 19 years 125 days

YOUNGEST WINNER

Sebastian Vettel (Germany) – 21 years 73 days

OLDEST STARTER

Louis Chiron (Monaco) – 55 years 292 days

OLDEST WINNER

Luigi Fagioli (Italy) – 53 years 22 days

MOST FASTEST LAPS IN CAREER

Michael Schumacher (Germany) – 77

MOST POLE POSITIONS

Michael Schumacher (Germany) – 68

World Champion Constructors 1958 – 2012

Year	Constructor (Drivers)
1958	Vanwall (GB) (Stirling Moss, Tony Brooks)
1959	Cooper (GB) (Jack Brabham, Stirling Moss, Bruce McLaren)
1960	Cooper (GB) (Jack Brabham, Bruce McLaren)
1961	Ferrari (Italy) (Phil Hill, Wolfgang von Trips)
1962	BRM (GB) (Graham Hill)
1963	Lotus (GB) (Jim Clark)
1964	Ferrari (Italy) (John Surtees, Lorenzo Bandini)
1965	Lotus (GB) (Jim Clark)
1966	Brabham (GB) (Jack Brabham)
1967	Brabham (GB) (Denny Hulme, Jack Brabham)
1968	Lotus (GB) (Graham Hill, Jo Siffert, Jim Clark, Jackie Oliver)
1969	Matra (France) (Jackie Stewart, Jean-Pierre Beltoise)
1970	Lotus (GB) (Jochen Rindt, Emerson Fittipaldi, Graham Hill, John Miles)
1971	Tyrrell (GB) (Jackie Stewart, François Cevert)
1972	Lotus (GB) (Emerson Fittipaldi)
1973	Lotus (GB) (Emerson Fittipaldi, Ronnie Peterson)
1974	McLaren (GB) (Emerson Fittipaldi, Denny Hulme, Mike Hailwood, David Hobbs, Jochen Mass)
1975	Ferrari (Italy) (Clay Regazzoni, Niki Lauda)
1976	Ferrari (Italy) (Niki Lauda, Clay Regazzoni)
1977	Ferrari (Italy) (Niki Lauda, Carlos Reutemann)
1978	Lotus (GB) (Mario Andretti, Ronnie Peterson)
1979	Ferrari (Italy) (Jody Scheckter, Gilles Villeneuve)
1980	Williams (GB) (Alan Jones, Carlos Reutemann)
1981	Williams (GB) (Alan Jones, Carlos Reutemann)
1982	Ferrari (Italy) (Gilles Villeneuve, Didier Pironi, Patrick Tambay, Mario Andretti)
1983	Ferrari (Italy) (Patrick Tambay, René Arnoux)
1984	McLaren (GB) (Alain Prost, Niki Lauda)
1985	McLaren (GB) (Niki Lauda, Alain Prost, John Watson)
1986	Williams (GB) (Nigel Mansell, Nelson Piquet)
1987	Williams (GB) (Nigel Mansell, Nelson Piquet)
1988	McLaren (GB) (Alain Prost, Ayrton Senna)
1989	McLaren (GB) (Ayrton Senna, Alain Prost)
1990	McLaren (GB) (Ayrton Senna, Gerhard Berger)
1991	McLaren (GB) (Ayrton Senna, Gerhard Berger)
1992	Williams (GB) (Nigel Mansell, Riccardo Patrese)
1993	Williams (GB) (Damon Hill, Alain Prost)
1994	Williams (GB) (Damon Hill, Ayrton Senna, David Coulthard, Nigel Mansell)
1995	Benetton (GB) (Michael Schumacher, Johnny Herbert)
1996	Williams (GB) (Damon Hill, Jacques Villeneuve)
1997	Williams (GB) (Jacques Villeneuve, Heinz-Harald Frentzen)
1998	McLaren (GB) (David Coulthard, Mika Häkkinen)
1999	Ferrari (Italy) (Michael Schumacher, Eddie Irvine, Mika Salo)
2000	Ferrari (Italy) (Michael Schumacher, Rubens Barrichello)
2001	Ferrari (Italy) (Michael Schumacher, Rubens Barrichello)
2002	Ferrari (Italy) (Michael Schumacher, Rubens Barrichello)
2003	Ferrari (Italy) (Michael Schumacher, Rubens Barrichello)
2004	Ferrari (Italy) (Michael Schumacher, Rubens Barrichello)
2005	Renault (France) (Fernando Alonso, Giancarlo Fisichella)
2006	Renault (France) (Fernando Alonso, Giancarlo Fisichella)
2007	Ferrari (Italy) (Felipe Massa, Kimi Räikkönen)
2008	Ferrari (Italy) (Kimi Räikkönen, Felipe Massa)
2009	Brawn (GB) (Jenson Button, Rubens Barrichello)
2010	Red Bull (Austria) (Sebastian Vettel, Mark Webber)
2011	Red Bull (Austria) (Sebastian Vettel, Mark Webber)
2012	Red Bull (Austria) (Sebastian Vettel, Mark Webber)

FERNANDO ALONSO

Widely acknowledged as one of the greatest Formula One drivers of all time, Ferrari's Fernando Alonso has worked wonders to remain Sebastian Vettel's fiercest rival despite his Italian team lacking the flat-out pace of Red Bull.

The Spaniard twice won the world championship with Renault, prevailing in successive years in 2005 and 2006. It was the culmination of a meteoric rise to the sport's pinnacle for Alonso, who made his debut in Australia for Minardi in 2001, aged only 19. Alonso totalled seven race victories in both his title-winning seasons, beating off fierce competition from Kimi Räikkönen and Michael Schumacher, before embarking on an unhappy spell at McLaren in 2007. He narrowly lost the title to Ferrari's Räikkönen in his first year, but was released by McLaren in 2008 after enduring a strained relationship with teammate Lewis Hamilton.

The 1999 Euro Open by Nissan champion, Alonso spent only two years racing professionally before moving into F1, which was a reflection of his staggering natural talent. This ability allowed him to exceed expectations in finishing fifth in 2008 for Renault and second in 2010 for Ferrari, after he was chosen to replace Räikkönen.

After that near-miss, 2011 was disappointing for Alonso, with a solitary victory in the British GP, but he rallied again to run Vettel's Red Bull right to the wire again in 2012. Alonso's 13 podiums meant victory in the final race in Brazil would secure the Spaniard an unlikely third world title. He finished second and lost to Vettel by three points.

FACT PANEL

BORN: July 29, 1981; Oviedo, Spain
2013 TEAM: Ferrari
DEBUT: 2001 Australian GP (Minardi)
FIRST F1 WIN: 2003 Hungarian GP (Renault)
FIRST F1 TITLE: 2005 (Renault)

FELIPE MASSA

A mixed recent record for Ferrari pales into insignificance for Felipe Massa, given the Brazilian's miraculous recovery to return to Formula One less than a year after sustaining life-threatening head injuries while practising at the 2009 Hungarian Grand Prix.

Although forced to play second fiddle to teammate Fernando Alonso since returning, Massa reached seven podiums between 2010 and 2012, registering sixth-place finishes in the drivers' championship in the first two years before coming seventh in 2012. Prior to the injury, Massa had been a leading force in F1 and was runner-up in 2008, with McLaren's Lewis Hamilton snatching fifth place in the Brazilian Grand Prix – a race won by Massa – to win the title by a single point.

It was the sixth race win of a very successful season for Massa, 12 months after he had frustratingly been outperformed by teammate Kimi Räikkönen. Indeed, Massa has revealed in performing well at his home Grand Prix. In 2006, he became the first Brazilian since Ayrton Senna to be victorious at Interlagos, sealing third spot in the standings in the process and registering a second career race victory.

That success came at the end of his first racing season for Ferrari, in which he pushed legendary new teammate Michael Schumacher and proved a worthy adversary to champion, and future Ferrari colleague, Fernando Alonso. The Italian team prised Massa away from Sauber in 2006, having used the Brazilian as a test driver in 2003 to add some maturity and experience to his natural ability. Having first been granted a race seat by Sauber in 2002, Massa performed respectably in 2004 and 2005, but only seriously competed for podiums after joining Ferrari.

FACT PANEL

BORN: April 25, 1981; São Paulo, Brazil
2013 TEAM: Ferrari
DEBUT: 2002 Australian GP (Sauber)
FIRST F1 WIN: 2006 Turkish GP (Ferrari)
BEST F1 SEASON: 2nd in 2008 (Ferrari)

JENSON BUTTON

Jenson Button will be intent on putting a frustrating period for himself and McLaren in the past by rediscovering the form that saw him win the 2009 drivers' championship and become the first teammate of Lewis Hamilton's to beat him in the standings.

Nobody has been more deserving of success in Formula One than Button, who endured an agonising six-year wait for a maiden race victory after first joining Williams in 2000. Both with them and Honda, Button lacked the racing pace to trouble the best in the sport, but finally ended his wait for a victory in Hungary in 2006.

His future was shrouded in doubt two years later, though, when Honda withdrew. But Button rose from the depths of despair to a maiden world championship in 12 months, thanks largely to Ross Brawn. His late buyout secured Button a place on the grid for 2009, under the name Brawn GP. Button had previously offered to take a £15m pay cut to keep Honda afloat in F1 so deserved the blistering pace the Brawn car, with its innovative diffuser design, offered him. He won six of the first seven races in 2009 to sew up the championship with a race to spare.

At McLaren, Button has not been able to match Sebastian Vettel but has answered doubters who feared the move would expose him as inferior to British rival Lewis Hamilton. He claimed eight race wins in his first three years at McLaren and beat Hamilton by finishing second in the standings in 2011. Button, who won karting competitions and the 1998 Formula Ford Championship before moving to F1, remains a contender for further titles.

FACT PANEL

BORN: January 19, 1980; Frome, England
2013 TEAM: McLaren
DEBUT: 2000 Australian Grand Prix (Williams)
FIRST F1 WIN: 2006 Hungarian Grand Prix (Honda)
FIRST F1 TITLE: 2009 (Brawn)

NICO ROSBERG

Nico Rosberg was surely destined for a career in motorsport; son of Formula One legend Keke, Lewis Hamilton's 2013 teammate last year holds dual Finnish and German nationality, arguably the most prolific nations in producing F1 champions.

He once pondered over pursuing a tennis career but ultimately opted for racing, a decision vindicated by early success in karting before he won the German Formula BMW in his debut season when aged 17. When he tested for the Williams team in 2002 he was the youngest person to drive an F1 car and in 2005 he won the inaugural GP2 series for ART.

Offered an F1 race seat by Williams for 2006, Rosberg started slowly before scoring 20 points and registering a ninth-place finish in the 2007 drivers' championship. He reached his first podiums in 2008, in Australia and Singapore, despite his Williams car generally lacking pace. Rosberg signed with Mercedes for the 2010 season, to drive alongside fellow German, the legendary Michael Schumacher.

Initially Rosberg struggled to match F1's pacesetters with Mercedes but he consistently outperformed Schumacher. At the 2012 Chinese Grand Prix he finally ended his wait for a maiden race victory, 24 hours after claiming his first pole position. His 20-second victory represented the first by a German driving a German car and the first Mercedes triumph since the legendary Juan Manual Fangio in 1955.

During the 2013 season Rosberg seemed to revel in being the latest teammate of 2008 world champion Lewis Hamilton. He claimed his second and third race victories and chose two of F1's most iconic venues to get them: Silverstone and Monaco.

FACT PANEL

BORN: June 27, 1985; Wiesbaden, Germany
2013 TEAM: Mercedes
DEBUT: 2006 Bahrain GP (Williams)
FIRST F1 WIN: 2012 Chinese GP (Mercedes)
BEST F1 SEASON: 7th in 2009 (Williams), 2010 and 2011 (both Mercedes)

01 Australia

Venue - Albert Park, Melbourne
Circuit length - 5.303km
Turns - 16 ▪ Laps - 58

Often the curtain-raiser of the Formula One season, Albert Park seems to have a special appeal for Finnish drivers, with victory there often auguring well for their seasons.

Kimi Raikkonen's win last year, his second in Australia, came six years after his maiden Melbourne triumph kick-started his 2007 title-winning season. His compatriot Mika Hakkinen won for McLaren in Australia in 1998 and also went on to win the World Championship that year.

Staged in Melbourne since 1996, the Australian Grand Prix has also been a happy hunting ground for Brits, with Jenson Button and David Coulthard both multiple winners Down Under.

The German Michael Schumacher boasts the most Melbourne wins, triumphing four times during his Ferrari days, while his 1'24.125 in 2004 is the record for the fastest racing lap time, although compatriot Sebastian Vettel recorded a quicker qualifying time in 2011.

The circuit, which circles Albert Park Lake, is regarded one of the easier tracks to navigate, owing to its consistent and regular corners, although overtaking is tricky with few lengthy straights to build up speed.

DID YOU KNOW?

The Adelaide Street Circuit held the Australian Grand Prix before Albert Park and was host to controversy in 1991 when Ayrton Senna won a race abandoned after 16 laps of 71 because of torrential rain, with drivers critical of the dangerous conditions. Second-placed Nigel Mansell could not take his place on the podium as he was recovering in hospital from a crash.

02 Malaysia

Venue - Sepang International Circuit, Sepang
Circuit length - 5.543km
Turns - 15 ▪ Laps - 56

Sepang in Malaysia has featured in Formula One since 1999 and the exciting circuit, packed with overtaking opportunities and twisting complexes, has become a firm drivers' favourite.

The track developed because the Malaysian Prime Minister, Dr Mahathir Mohamad, wanted the nation to industrialise rapidly through car manufacturing. An offshoot of this was a Formula One facility that aimed to be the envy of the world.

The Malaysian Grand Prix dates back to 1962 but it was only the concerted investment in the country's motor industry that brought Formula One to the country.

Sebastian Vettel's victory last year was his third at Sepang, equalling the number won by his fellow German Michael Schumacher for Ferrari.

The Italian giants have warmed to Sepang, winning six of the venue's 13 races, although their current driver Fernando Alonso's three Malaysia wins were each sealed with a different constructor.

DID YOU KNOW?

The 2009 Malaysian Grand Prix was special for two reasons. The night race was abandoned 31 laps into the 56-lap even because of torrential rain, meaning half points were allocated to drivers for the first time in 18 years. Secondly, Jenson Button's victory meant Brawn GP won their first two races, the first constructor to achieve that feat since the 1980s.

03 China

Venue – Shanghai International Circuit, Shanghai
Circuit length – 5.451km
Turns – 16 ▪ Laps – 56

Set to host its 11th Grand Prix in 2014, the Shanghai International Circuit has proved a fine addition to the Formula One calendar after a $450m investment transformed disused marshland into one of the best tracks on the circuit.

A fantastic combination of winding turns and long high-speed straights – including the largest in F1 – places high demands on the drivers but provides gripping viewing for spectators, never more so than in 2005 when Shanghai hosted the season's last race. World Champion Fernando Alonso – who won for the second time in China last year – led the way to hand Renault the Constructor's Championship.

Victory in China also proved key for McLaren's Lewis Hamilton in 2008, leaving him on the cusp of his maiden World Championship, and the Englishman replicated his Shanghai success in 2011. Kimi Raikkonen was also victorious in China en route to the title, in 2007; that win was Ferrari's 200th in Formula One.

Fears have surfaced regarding falling attendances and rumours parts of the track are sinking, but Shanghai has been commercially successful. Architects Hermann Tilke and Peter Wahl tried to combine China's increasing modernity with its history, a typical example being how state-of-the-art facilities are contained in team buildings arranged like pavilions in a lake, to resemble Shanghai's ancient Yuyan-Garden.

DID YOU KNOW?

Originally, the Zhuhai International Circuit was destined to host Formula One in China. It was even included in the provisional calendar for 1999, only to be denied a race after failing to meet FIA safety standards.

04 Bahrain

Venue – Bahrain International Circuit, Sakhir
Circuit length – 5.412km
Turns – 15 ▪ Laps – 57

Sebastian Vettel has not allowed safety concerns in Bahrain to deflect his attentions from accruing championship points – the prolific German has won two years running at Sakhir since the 2011 instalment of the race was cancelled amidst a civil uprising.

Off-track controversies aside, Bahrain has played host to exciting racing since its addition to the calendar in 2004. Fernando Alonso will certainly hope calls for Bahrain to be axed from the calendar never materialise: the Spaniard has won three of the nine races staged there.

The 15-turn circuit provides three genuine overtaking opportunities, partly due to the variation in the track's width. The generous run-off areas have been criticised for not punishing driving mistakes but they do prevent sand from the surrounding desert reaching the track.

There are also very wide sections owing to the venue being built for flexibility – indeed there are five track layouts within the same grid, the Formula One track being accompanied by an endurance circuit – used for the 2010 Grand Prix – as well as a testing oval and drag strip.

Thirty miles south-west of Bahrain's capital, Manama, the circuit became the first to stage Formula One racing in the Middle East.

DID YOU KNOW?

Despite the respective countries being separated by more than 3,000 miles, a third of the 12,000 tons of stone used to build the Bahrain track was Welsh granite. It was chosen for its excellent adhesive qualities.

50 Years Ago - 1964

British drivers dominated the 1960s in Formula One, with six of the nation's 14 world championships coming during that golden era. In 1964 it was the turn of John Surtees, who made history when he pipped 1962 champion and fellow Brit Graham Hill by a single point.

Surtees had been a multiple world motorcycle racing champion in the 1950s, when he became the first man to win the senior Isle of Man TT three times in a row. He switched to four wheels in 1960 and his title triumph made him the first – and only – man to win world championships on motorcycles and in cars.

He joined Scuderia Ferrari in 1963 and led the team in 1964 alongside Lorenzo Bandini, taking on the Lotus-Climax of reigning British world champion Jim Clark and Hill's BRM.

When Clark won the British Grand Prix – held for the first time at Brands Hatch – for the third consecutive time, Hill and Surtees were second and third but the title looked to be between Clark and Hill.

But then Surtees won two of the next three races, at the Nurburgring (German) and Monza (Italian), before finishing second to Hill in the United States GP at Watkins Glen.

As the 10-race season reached its finale in Mexico, Hill had a five-point lead over Surtees with Clark a further four points back in third. A collision with Bandini put Hill out of points contention and Clark, who had led from the outset, looked set for the title with two laps to go. But then his engine seized, handing the lead to the American Dan Gurney in his Brabham-Climax. Waves through by Bandini, Surtees finished second, which was enough for him to take the title.

The Ferrari Story

The history of Ferrari in motor racing is all about Scuderia Ferrari, the racing division of the Ferrari automobile manufacturer. The Italian team is the most successful in the history of Formula One team with a record of 15 drivers' championships and 16 constructors' championships.

But while Scuderia Ferrari is identified mainly with Formula One, the team goes back to its formation by Enzo Ferrari in 1929, including sports car racing. As well as the most successful, it is the oldest name in motorsport, having competed since 1932, when the famous prancing horse badge appeared for the first time in the Spa 24 Hours race.

Enzo Ferrari brought together his stable of drivers initially to race cars produced by Alfa Romeo, though by the 1940s he was developing cars of his own. When his association with Alfa Romeo ended, he founded AAC (Auto Avio Costruzioni) to manufacture aircraft parts for the Italian government, but he was also commissioned by the Marquis of Modena to build a racing car. The two AAC Tipo 815s that made their debut in the 1940 Brescia Grand Prix are regarded by some as the first Ferrari cars.

But legal issues connected with the Alfa Romeo split at first prevented Enzo Ferrari from running a car bearing his own name and it was not until 1947 that he was able to unveil the first racing car designed and built at the Ferrari factory in Modena, northern Italy.

This was the Ferrari 125S that made its debut at

Piacenza on May 11. Driven by Franco Cortese, the car failed to finish the race but 14 days later came home first at the Grand Prix of Rome, again driven by Cortese, who thus became Ferrari's first winning driver.

Since then, Alberto Ascari, Juan Manuel Fangio, Mike Hawthorn, Phil Hill, John Surtees, Niki Lauda, Jody Scheckter, Michael Schumacher and Kimi Räikkönen have all become world champions while driving for the Ferrari team.

When Formula One was launched in 1950, Ferrari took part in the second race, the Monaco Grand Prix, and Ascari finished second in the 125 F1 behind Juan Manuel Fangio's Alfa Romeo. Ascari finished fifth in the standings, with the Alfas in the first three places. Italy's Giuseppe Farina was the first world champion.

But it did not take long for Ferrari to break Alfa's grip. The following year the Argentinian Jose Froilan Gonzales became Ferrari's first Formula One winner when he drove the 375 F1 to victory at Silverstone. Ascari won the German and Italian GPs and though Fangio took the drivers' title, the Ferraris finished second and third in the standings, pushing Farina down to fourth.

Alberto Ascari

Juan Manuel Fangio

Mike Hawthorn

In 1952, Ferrari won the title for the first time as Ascari finished first in every race he completed, retaining the championship in 1953, when there were also Ferrari wins for Britain's Mike Hawthorn and for Farina, who had moved from Alfa Romeo.

Fangio took the upper hand again for the next four years – driving a Ferrari in 1956 – and Hawthorn won the title in 1958 to become the first British champion but it was a bittersweet season for Ferrari as drivers Peter Collins and Luigi Musso were killed. Hawthorn retired from the sport only to be killed himself when he crashed his Jaguar on the Guildford bypass.

The 1960s saw American Phil Hill help Ferrari to a first constructors' crown in 1961 but his own drivers' title was overshadowed as teammate and rival Wolfgang von Trips was killed in the title-decider at Monza. Former motorcycle racer John Surtees won for Ferrari in 1964 to become the only man to win world titles on two and four wheels.

This was an era dominated by British drivers, with Surtees, Jim Clark, Graham Hill and Jackie Stewart winning eight World Championships between them in 12 years. Ferrari would not provide another title-winning driver until 1975, when the Austrian Niki Lauda powered the 312T, with a transversal gearbox that enabled better weight distribution, to five wins and eight podium finishes.

The remarkable Lauda, who had won the Scuderia's 50th Formula One GP in 1974, suffered serious burns in an accident at the 1976 German GP but still lost the title by only a point to James Hunt and won it back in 1977. South Africa's Jody Scheckter claimed the 1979 title but he was Ferrari's last champion until 2000, with the next two decades dominated by Williams and McLaren.

Ferrari won two constructors' championships in the 1980s but the early part of the decade was marred by the death in 1982 of main driver Gilles Villeneuve during practice for the Belgian GP. Then, in 1988, Enzo Ferrari himself passed away at the age of 90.

The 1990s began promisingly with Alain Prost finishing second in the drivers' championship in the Ferrari 641 but Scuderia could not build on that success and in 1996 came the momentous decision to hire the German Michael Schumacher, world champion two years in a row for Benetton, on what was considered an astronomical salary of around $30 million a year. Schumacher also brought with him the nucleus of his Benetton team, including technical director Ross Brawn and chief designer Rory Byrne.

Phil Hill

John Surtees

Michael Schumacher

Michael Schumacher

Fernando Alonso

Felipe Massa

Kimi Raikonnen

Niki Lauda

Jody Scheckter

The rebuilding process took time but Schumacher was second to the McLaren-Mercedes of Mika Häkkinen in 1998 after winning six races and teammate Eddie Irvine runner-up in 1999 after Schumacher had broken his leg in a crash at Silverstone and missed seven races.

Schumacher turned the tables on the Finn Häkkinen in 2000 in the Ferrari F1-2000, winning nine races from 17 and giving the Scuderia their first drivers' champion for 21 years. It began a period of dominance by Schumacher, who was to hold the title for five years in a row, and Ferrari, who took the constructors' crown six years on the spin.

Twice Schumacher set a new record for winning points margin, finishing 58 points clear of his rivals after achieving nine victories and five second places in 2001, then 67 points in front in 2002, when he won a record 11 Grand Prix and clinched the title at the earliest point in F1 history, with still six races to go. With Rubens Barrichello winning four times, Ferrari's dominance was such that they won 15 of 17 races, taking the constructors' championship with a mammoth 221 points, as many as the other 10 teams put together.

The 2003 campaign was much closer, the winning margin just two points. But Schumacher recovered a deficit on 16 points at one stage to win a nip-and-tuck battle with Kimi Räikkönen's McLaren-Mercedes, setting another record with his sixth championship, passing Fangio's five.

Records were smashed in 2004 as Schumacher won 12 of the first 13 races and clinching a record seventh drivers' title at the Belgian Grand Prix, finishing the season with a record 148 points, 34 points ahead of the runner-up, teammate Rubens Barrichello, and

a record 13 race wins out of a possible 18. With Barrichello winning two of the last four GPs, Ferrari won 15 races in total, including eight one-twos, and 262 points in the constructors' championship.

The Scuderia's car was much less competitive under 2005 tyre regulations and Schumacher's win at the United States GP was Ferrari's only success. There was a substantial recovery in 2006, when Schumacher announced he would retire at the end of the season after winning at Monza in September. The German wanted to go out as champion and led the standings after finishing first in the next race, in China. But he missed out in the end to Fernando Alonso, despite going out with an heroic effort in the final GP in Brazil, when he fought back from 19th place to finish fourth.

In 180 GPs with Ferrari, Schumacher won 72 races, gained 58 pole positions, drove 53 fastest race laps and won five drivers' and six constructors' titles.

After Schumacher, the Scuderia claimed its 15th drivers' title after an intense battle with McLaren when Kimi Räikkönen beat Lewis Hamilton by a single point in 2007, the Finn pipping the rookie British driver in the final race of the season in Brazil. Ferrari took the constructors' title with nine wins (six to Räikkönen, three to Felipe Massa) after McLaren were disqualified amid an espionage controversy, retaining it in 2008 despite Hamilton clinching the drivers' crown.

Ferrari drivers were runners-up three times in five years after Räikkönen's victory, Massa to Hamilton in 2008 and Fernando Alonso behind Sebastian Vettel in 2010 and 2012 as the Spaniard developed a running duel with the new German world champion that continued in 2013.

ROMAIN GROSJEAN

Grosjean, born in Geneva but a French national, has quickly adapted to being a regular points scorer in Formula One since being handed his first permanent place on the grid as Kimi Räikkönen's understudy at Lotus.

His route to F1 was traditional. He was the Swiss Formula Renault 1600 champion in 2003, the French Formula Renault winner in 2005 and, racing for ASM, won the Formula Three Euro series at the second attempt after winning six races in 2007, by which point he had secured a place on Renault's driver development programme.

Upon graduating to GP2 in 2008, Grosjean won the inaugural GP2 Asia series with ART while testing in F1 for the first time with Renault. Installed as the French team's third driver, he was granted a race seat on the grid sooner than anticipated when Nelson Piquet Jr's contract was cancelled but, after seven indifferent races, Renault opted against retaining him for the 2010 season.

Showing the heart and belief of a winner, Grosjean rebuilt his confidence away from F1. Back in GP2 in 2011, he excelled, winning both the Asian and the main series after scoring six victories, success which prompted an F1 return in 2012 as a Lotus driver. Several podiums, two of which have come in Bahrain, and a host of top-ten finishes have justified Lotus' judgement.

FACT PANEL

BORN: April 17, 1986; Geneva, Switzerland
2013 TEAM: Lotus
DEBUT: 2009 European GP (Renault)
BEST F1 RACE: 2nd in 2012 Canadian GP (Lotus)
BEST F1 SEASON: 2012 (Lotus)

SERGIO PEREZ

Sergio Perez, the first Mexican since Hector Rabaque retired in 1981 to race in Formula One, will be desperate for more pace and points after he was selected to replace Lewis Hamilton at McLaren in 2013.

His debut on the grid for Sauber in Bahrain came only two years before the move to the iconic British team.

McLaren showed faith in Perez's ability despite his failure to win a race with Sauber, although he did reach three podiums in 2012. In Malaysia he ran Fernando Alonso close for victory while at Monza he overtook the Spaniard, Kimi Räikkönen and Felipe Massa, on both occasions finishing second. His efforts at Sepang earned Sauber a maiden podium finish.

Perez made his single-seater bow in the 2004 Skip Barber National championship in the United States, with financial backing from Escuderia Telmex, which supports racing drivers.

Moving to Europe, he finished 14th in Germany's Formula BMW ADAC series in 2005 and 6th in 2006, before stepping up to the national class of British Formula Three, winning the title and promotion to international class for 2008, when he achieved four wins to finish 4th overall.

He finished 7th in his first Asian GP2 series before enjoying a hugely successful 2010 campaign in the main GP2 series, driving for Barwa Addax, collecting five wins and seven podiums only to finish narrowly runner-up to Pastor Maldonado. That fine return won him a seat with Sauber for 2011 before he had even tested in F1.

FACT PANEL

BORN: January 26, 1990; Guadalajara, Mexico
2013 TEAM: McLaren
DEBUT: 2011 Australian GP (Sauber)
BEST F1 RACE: 2nd in 2012 Malaysian GP (Sauber)
BEST F1 SEASON: 16th in 2011 (Sauber)

DANIEL RICCIARDO

Just half a season of test driving was enough to persuade Toro Rosso to grant Daniel Ricciardo his first race seat in Formula One and the Australian inspired by Ayrton Senna to take up motorsport is now a regular among the points.

Ricciardo made his single-seater debut in Australian Formula Ford in 2005, impressing adequately in a 15-year-old Van Diemen to earn a scholarship for the following season's Formula BMW Asia championship, in which he finished 3rd with the Eurasia team.

In 2007 he raced in Italian Formula Renault, ending the season 6th, before landing his first title the following year in the Formula Renault Western European Cup with eight wins from 15 races. In 2009 he made another advance, winning the British Formula Three title. He was by this time a member of the Red Bull junior team and made his track debut in an F1 car at a young drivers test in December. He became the regular third driver for Toro Rosso after a runner-up finish in the Formula Renault 3.5 series in 2010.

He impressed so much there was immediate talk of a race seat but Red Bull opted to allow him to continue his development in 3.5 racing while driving for HRT from the midway point of the 2011 season onwards. Although he picked up no points with them, his performances were competent enough to secure a permanent drive with Toro Rosso for 2012.

FACT PANEL

BORN: July 1, 1989; Perth, Australia
2013 TEAM: Toro Rosso
DEBUT: 2011 British GP (HRT)
BEST F1 RACE: 7th in 2013 Chinese GP (Sauber)
BEST F1 SEASON: 18th in 2012 (Toro Rosso)

JEAN-ERIC VERGNE

One of a clutch of promising young French drivers, Jean-Eric Vergne has threatened to become a serious contender towards the front of the F1 grid.

The Parisian graduated from karting to single-seater car racing in 2007, joining the French Formula Campus series and winning the title with six victories and was soon invited to join Red Bull's young driver programme, which enabled him to compete in both the Eurocup Formula Renault 2.0 and West European Cup in 2008.

In 2010 he made a highly successful transition to British Formula Three, winning the prestigious title at the first attempt in 2010 with an impressive 13 victories. He made his Formula One test debut with Toro Rosso in November of the same year and also took part in four GP3 races. The following year, he finished runner-up in the Formula Renault 3.5 series and drove for Toro Rosso during first free practice at three of the last four Grands Prix.

Impressive displays at a young driver test after the Abu Dhabi GP in November of the same year, posting a lap time only half a second behind Sebastian Vettel's pole time, Vergne landed an F1 race drive for the 2012 season with Toro Rosso. Despite a host of retirements and some predictable early race disappointments, Vergne now looks a driver ready to make a big impact in F1.

FACT PANEL

BORN: April 25, 1990; Pontoise, France
2013 TEAM: Toro Rosso
DEBUT: 2012 Australian GP (Toro Rosso)
BEST F1 RACE: 6th in 2013 Canadian GP (Toro Rosso)
BEST F1 SEASON: 17th in 2012 (Toro Rosso)

40 Years Ago - 1974

The 1974 season was the 25th in Formula One and produced a fittingly thrilling battle for the title in which Brazil's Emerson Fittipaldi and the Swiss driver Clay Regazzoni went into the last race of the world championship level on points.

In a winter of major changes, Fittipaldi had quit Lotus to join McLaren, who had substantial new backing from Texaco and Marlboro, while Regazzoni had rejoined Ferrari after a year at BRM, taking the Austrian Niki Lauda with him.

After Fittipaldi's teammate, the New Zealander Denny Hulme, had won the first of the 15 races in Argentina, Fittipaldi won on home soil in Brazil and scored his second victory in Belgium. Lauda, who qualified in pole position nine times, won two races to Regazzoni's one but the latter's consistent points scoring kept him in the hunt for the title. He made good ground in July and August as Fittipaldi failed to finish three races in four, during which time Regazzoni scored his one victory in Germany and picked up points in his three other races.

Fittipaldi won the penultimate race, the Canadian Grand Prix, at Mosport, Ontario, beating Regazzoni into second place and they went into the final race at Watkin's Glen in New York on equal points. It did not go well for Regazzoni, who developed handling problems and dropped down the field. Fittipaldi finished only fourth, but it was enough to take the title – his second in three years – by three points.

The race was marred by the death of Helmuth Koinigg, an Austrian rookie, who became the second fatality of the season after America's Peter Revson was killed in practice at the South African GP in March.

05 Spain

Venue - Valencia Street Circuit
Circuit length - 5.419km
Turns - 25 • Laps - 57

Despite its relatively young age, the 2008-built Valencia Street Circuit will be hosting its second different Formula One event in 2014 when it hosts the Spanish Grand Prix for the first time.

Designed by prolific track architect Hermann Tilke, the circuit was host of the European Grand Prix for five straight years until the event was axed from the F1 calendar in 2012. It occupies a prime waterside position, with part of the track crossing a canal.

With long, narrow straights and limited run-off areas, Valencia has been criticised for a lack of overtaking opportunities, although the change to Pirelli tyres and the introduction of DRS in 2011 saw passing figures improve at the circuit before it was removed from the 2013 calendar.

Ferrari's Felipe Massa won the inaugural Valencia event in 2008 and Fernando Alonso was victorious the last time Formula One ventured there, with Sebastian Vettel claiming back-to-back triumphs in his title-winning seasons of 2010 and 2011.

DID YOU KNOW?

In the 2012 European Grand Prix at Valencia, third-placed Michael Schumacher, at 43 years and 173 days, became the oldest man to reach the podium at a Grand Prix since Jack Brabham at the British Grand Prix in 1970. It was also the last podium finish of Schumacher's illustrious career.

06 Monaco

Venue - Circuit de Monaco, Monte Carlo
Circuit length - 3.340km
Turns - 19 • Laps - 78

One of the most famous races in motorsport, the Monaco Grand Prix continues to see off competition from expensive new facilities to remain the highlight of the Formula One calendar.

The charming Monte Carlo circuit has barely changed its configuration since it first hosted Formula One racing in 1955 and requires precise car control and significant bravery from victorious drivers.

Nico Rosberg's victory last year in a race littered with crashes and bumps fittingly summed up the chaos which can rule in Monte Carlo. The great Ayrton Senna seemed to relish the challenge; his six Monaco victories are the most of any driver and include five in succession between 1989 and 1993.

Jenson Button – who, like many drivers, lives in Monte Carlo – is among a string of Britons to taste glory in Monaco. Multiple winners are Stirling Moss and Jackie Stewart with three triumphs apiece while Graham Hill won five times during the 1960s.

The race actually predates Formula One, having been staged first in 1929, and has become almost as well known for the celebrities it attracts as the racing, with Brad Pitt, Roman Abramovich and George Clooney among recent visitors on race weekends.

DID YOU KNOW?

After Michael Schumacher, Jean Alesi and Damon Hill all retired while leading, the 1996 Monaco Grand Prix was won by Olivier Panis – who started 14th on the grid – with only two other drivers finishing. The victory was the only race win of the Frenchman's career.

07 Canada

Venue – Circuit Gilles Villeneuve, Montreal
Circuit length – 4.361km
Turns – 14 ▪ Laps – 70

Known as the Gilles Villeneuve Circuit since the death of the Canadian great in 1982, Montreal's famous track has hosted its country's Grand Prix every year since the late 1970s, apart from 2009 when it was not held.

Prior to the Ile Notre-Dame circuit's construction, Canada's French and English parts of Montreal had alternated Formula One races between them. When the Mont-Tremblant track was deemed too dangerous, Canadians from the French region opted to take ownership of the race with a brand new track.

Fittingly, Villeneuve won the first Grand Prix at the circuit but he remains the only Canadian to have won at the new track. Michael Schumacher has seven victories at Montreal – the most of any driver – including six for Ferrari, the constructor with the most wins (10) in Montreal.

The 2008 instalment was particularly special; Robert Kubica's victory is his only one in Formula One to date while the triumph also represented the only win and 1-2 finish for BMW Sauber, who left the sport in 2009.

Last year's Canadian Grand Prix, won by Sebastian Vettel, was tarnished by the death of a marshal at the end of the race, the first tragedy of its kind in 12 years.

DID YOU KNOW?

Jenson Button's thrilling 2011 win in Canada was a long time in the making; the Briton overtook Sebastian Vettel only on the last lap after starting seventh on the grid. The race was also the longest in F1 history – at four hours, four minutes and 39 seconds – due to a lengthy rain delay.

08 Great Britain

Venue – Silverstone Circuit, Northamptonshire
Circuit length – 5.891km
Turns – 18 ▪ Laps – 52

The centre of British motorsport, Silverstone will host its 50th British Grand Prix in 2014, 48 of which have been Formula One races.

The circuit, located near the Northamptonshire-Buckinghamshire border, first hosted the British Grand Prix in 1948 and has scarcely altered in its appearance since it first staged a Formula One weekend in 1950.

Silverstone has been the sole host of the British Formula One weekend since 1987 but had previously shared the honour with two tracks. From 1955 to 1962, it alternated with Aintree before the Merseyside venue fell out of favour, after which Kent's Brands Hatch reached an agreement to stage the race biennially until the mid 1980s.

French legend Alain Prost felt at home across the channel at Silverstone, winning in 1983, 1985, 1989, 1990 and 1993. 12 British drivers have won at the rural track, Lewis Hamilton the most recent in his title-winning season of 2008. Nigel Mansell also won Silverstone en route to being crowned world champion – in 1992 – and he and Jim Clark are the only Britons to have won at both Silverstone and Brands Hatch.

Silverstone's grip on the British Grand Prix was challenged in 2008 by Donington Park. A tentative agreement was reached for the Leicestershire track to host Formula One racing from 2010 but rights were returned to Silverstone when funding for Donington fell through.

DID YOU KNOW?

As well as the British Grand Prix, Silverstone hosted eight other major motorsport events in 2013, including Formula 3 and World Superbike meetings.

Lewis Hamilton

The decision to up sticks and leave McLaren in 2012 was not one Lewis Hamilton will have taken lightly. The British team helped him to the 2008 world drivers' championship, having nurtured his development since the age of 13.

Now approaching 30, Hamilton joined Mercedes, after Michael Schumacher's second retirement opened the door for the move, in the hope it would allow him to loosen Sebastian Vettel's current stranglehold on Formula One.

From a very young age, the Hertfordshire-born Hamilton has shown a winning mentality, securing the British Cadet kart championship aged only 10 – the youngest ever to do so – before winning the Formula Three Euroseries and GP2 championships on his way to Formula One.

When Hamilton continued this run of titles at a tender age by securing the biggest one of all in 2008, few were surprised. In only his second year at the top level, Hamilton became the youngest ever F1 world champion, a record since broken by nemesis Vettel.

Then 23, Hamilton clinching the title on the final weekend in Brazil. He famously nabbed the fifth place finish he required to pip Felipe Massa to the title on the final corner of the last lap. His remarkable efforts were rewarded by the Queen with an MBE in the 2009 New Year honours.

Hamilton first signed for McLaren as an addition to their young driver programme in 1998 and was catapulted to the top as world champion Fernando Alonso's teammate in 2007. The confident young man dominated his more celebrated Spanish colleague in leading the drivers' championship for much of the season, winning four races and in the end losing the title to Ferrari's Kimi Räikkönen by a single point.

A steady decline in competitiveness for McLaren and some race frustrations for Hamilton have ensured he is yet to replicate the success of 2008. Hamilton has not had the luxury of the Red

Bull car available to Vettel, yet his attacking, racing instincts have ensured he remains one of the hardest drivers to beat.

Former McLaren teammate Jenson Button claimed Hamilton's World Championship crown from him in 2009, before becoming the first teammate to finish ahead of Hamilton in the standings in 2011. A host of frustrating accidents, tactical team errors and team tensions led to Hamilton's much-anticipated move to Mercedes in 2012.

FACT PANEL

BORN: January 7, 1985; Stevenage, England
2013 TEAM: Mercedes
DEBUT: 2007 Australian GP (McLaren)
FIRST F1 WIN: 2007 Canadian GP (McLaren)
FIRST F1 TITLE: 2008 (McLaren)

ADRIAN SUTIL

The Formula One career of Adrian Sutil appeared at a crossroads when Force India opted to replace him and fellow German Nico Hulkenberg in 2011.

After returning to the sport with the same manufacturer last year, Sutil has replicated the form he displayed in achieving a career-best ninth position in the drivers' standings in 2011. Indeed Sutil's F1 record for Force India has been relatively consistent, although an elusive maiden race victory still eluded him in his first six seasons.

Spyker – previously known as MF1 Racing – handed Sutil his first opportunity among motorsport's elite in 2006 as a test driver. He impressed them so much they granted Sutil his first race seat the following year and, after initial struggles, he scored his first championship point at the 2007 Japanese Grand Prix.

Prior to entering F1, Sutil cut his teeth in very similar fashion to most drivers on the grid. He raced in karting as a junior and starred in Formula Three as a teammate of Lewis Hamilton's at the ASM team in 2005. The Brit won the championship that season but Sutil came a close second and proved Hamilton's only serious competitor.

FACT PANEL

BORN: January 11, 1983; Starnberg, West Germany
2013 TEAM: Force India
DEBUT: 2007 Australian GP (Spyker)
BEST FORMULA ONE RACE: 4th in 2009 Italian GP (Force India)
BEST F1 SEASON: 9th in 2011 (Force India)

ESTEBAN GUTIERREZ

In joining compatriot Sergio Perez on the Formula One grid, Esteban Gutierrez became only the sixth Mexican to race in the sport and, with a very impressive record in other disciplines, can dream of becoming his country's first world champion.

Gutierrez won the Formula BMW Europe title in 2008 and joined ART Grand Prix to compete in the 2010 GP3 series, which he won after registering five race victories. The former of those two titles actually enabled him to drive an F1 car for the first time; BMW Sauber allowed him a test drive as a prize for his success.

The Mexican first competed in GP2 racing with Lotus in 2011, partnering fellow new boy in F1 Jules Bianchi, and Gutierrez finished third in his second GP2 campaign in 2012. Both years, he combined that work with his duties as a test driver for Sauber. When his countryman Perez left for McLaren, Gutierrez was selected to partner Nico Hulkenberg for the 2013 season.

Perez has been prominent throughout Gutierrez's short period in F1. He almost made his debut in June 2011 when Perez was unwell at the Canadian Grand Prix, still feeling the effects of a crash in Monaco. As test driver, the spot was rightfully Gutierrez's but, as he was in Mexico, Sauber were forced to call upon Pedro de la Rosa instead.

Gutierrez performed the best of all the 2013 rookies at the Australian GP last year but struggled to make a sizeable impact early in the season. He truly displayed his natural ability for the first time in F1 at the Spanish Grand Prix. After testing jostles with the likes of Jenson Button and Daniel Ricciardo, he finished only three tenths of a second behind the final points-scoring position and set the fastest lap of the race.

FACT PANEL

BORN: August 5, 1991; Monterrey, Mexico
2013 TEAM: Sauber
DEBUT: 2013 Australian GP (Sauber)
BEST FORMULA ONE RACE: 11th in 2013 Spanish GP (Sauber)
BEST GP3 SERIES SEASON: 1st in 2010 (ART Grand Prix)

VALTTERI BOTTAS

Valtteri Bottas is the latest in a long line of Finns to star in Formula One and, while he has significant work to do before he can dream of adding his name to those of Mika Häkkinen, Kimi Räikkönen and Keke Rosberg by becoming Finland's fourth World Champion, winning has proved something of a habit in his career so far.

Bottas, who raced for Williams in 2013 after working for them as a test driver for three seasons, has been a winner throughout his racing days. In 2011 he combined his work in F1 with a GP3 Series campaign, winning the championship with Lotus ART. Notably, he produced his best form when under pressure, winning four of the last seven meetings of the season to pip Brit James Calado to the crown.

Prior to that, the Finn twice won the Formula Three Masters title, in 2009 and 2010, and in the same years finished third twice in the Formula Three Euro series. In 2008, at the age of only 19, Bottas dominated Formula Renault racing, winning both the Eurocup and Northern European Cup.

Despite such a strong pedigree as a winner, it was still mildly surprising that Williams took a punt on the Finnish test driver to partner Venezuelan Pastor Maldonado in 2013. He repaid their faith with some solid performances. Notably he finished third in qualifying for last year's Canadian Grand Prix, with only Sebastian Vettel and Lewis Hamilton recording faster laps.

FACT PANEL

BORN: August 28, 1989; Nastola, Finland
2013 TEAM: Williams
DEBUT: 2013 Australian GP (Williams)
BEST FORMULA ONE RACE: 11th in 2013 Malaysian GP (Williams)
BEST GP3 SERIES SEASON: 1st in 2011 (Lotus ART)

JULES BIANCHI

Frenchman Jules Bianchi deserved the Formula One chance handed to him by Marussia last year after a career spent almost entirely competing for top honours in various motorsport disciplines.

Bianchi's impact on F1, having worked with Force India in 2012 as a test driver, has been limited but he has regularly outperformed teammate Max Chilton in competing well with Marussia's closest rivals Caterham. Great things could yet await Bianchi, who worked with Ferrari as a test driver in 2011.

Born in the south coast city of Nice, Bianchi has ancestors who were prominent in racing circles. Grandfather Mauro was world champion in GT racing three times while great uncle Lucien won the 1968 24 Hours of Le Mans and started 19 Formula One Grands Prix, finishing third in Monaco in 1968.

Bianchi's first serious racing assignment came in 2007 when he competed in the French Formula Renault 2.0. He won the title with five race victories, showing similar form which helped him finish third and first respectively in the 2008 and 2009 Formula Three Euro Series seasons.

Before entering F1, Bianchi proved his credentials in the tough breeding grounds of GP2 racing and the Formula Renault 3.5 series. By finishing third twice in GP2 and being the 2012 3.5 runner-up, he left himself perfectly prepared to make the final step up.

FACT PANEL

BORN: August 3, 1989; Nice, France
2013 TEAM: Marussia
DEBUT: 2013 Australian GP (Marussia)
BEST FORMULA ONE RACE: 13th in 2013 Malaysian GP (Marussia)
BEST FORMULA RENAULT 3.5 SEASON: 2nd in 2012 (Tech 1 Racing)

30 Years Ago - 1984

The 1984 season in Formula One was remarkable as the year that marked the beginning of McLaren's dominance – their drivers would win seven titles in eight years – and for another amazing achievement by Niki Lauda, the Austrian driver, who had won his second world championship in 1977 despite suffering horrific burns the previous year and now came out of retirement to win a third.

Lauda, needing money to support the charter airline he had set up after quitting the sport in 1979, returned to F1 in 1982 and showed he had lost none of his guile, winning twice on the way to fifth place. The following year was less successful but in 1984, with the TAG-Porsche engine up to speed and the return to McLaren of the Frenchman Alain Prost after his fall-out with Ferrari, everything changed.

came in the final race, the Portuguese GP in Estoril, where Prost won the race from the front row but Lauda fought his way through the field from 11th to finish second, pipping the Frenchman to the title by just half a point.

In a titanic battle between the two, Prost regularly outpaced Lauda in qualifying. But the canny Austrian, realising he could not beat Prost on speed, focussed instead on his race strategies. He did not achieve a single pole position all season but won races when Prost hit trouble and scored consistently when Prost's superior speed prevailed.

He had some luck on his side. Prost won seven races to Lauda's five but received only half the normal nine points for a win when the Monaco GP was stopped at the halfway stage due to heavy rain. However, a demonstration of Lauda's skill

Champions Wordsearch

Find the names of 18 Formula One venues hidden in this grid.

M	A	G	N	O	E	Y	S	Z	M	B	T	L	G
A	K	N	A	W	N	H	K	I	X	T	G	Z	R
K	T	S	F	P	A	X	E	K	E	H	R	F	O
U	S	B	A	N	S	H	M	A	N	S	E	C	K
Z	P	I	G	K	N	M	U	T	R	I	A	T	U
U	V	H	L	E	H	S	Z	N	U	N	T	J	A
S	A	Z	K	V	T	I	T	W	O	G	E	R	L
I	F	C	H	I	E	M	R	M	B	A	R	M	A
J	O	X	N	R	R	R	D	V	L	P	N	X	L
H	B	U	D	A	P	E	S	T	E	O	O	A	U
I	B	A	H	D	U	B	A	T	M	R	I	Z	M
J	T	S	A	O	P	A	U	L	O	E	D	N	P
L	Z	D	Y	N	K	N	K	Z	Y	N	A	O	U
L	A	E	R	T	N	O	M	T	H	Y	E	M	R

Melbourne	Shanghai	SaoPaulo	Monza
Hockenheim	Montreal	Sakhir	Singapore
Budapest	Spa	GreaterNoida	AbuDhabi
Silverstone	Suzuka	Austin	
KualaLumpur	Monaco	Yeongam	

Answers on page 60

33

Twenty Questions

1 Sebastian Vettel started his 100th Formula One race at the United States Grand Prix in 2012, finishing second to which British driver?

2 Lewis Hamilton finished second in the drivers' championship in his 2007 debut season in Formula One. How many races did he win?

3 Silverstone has been home to the British Grand Prix since 1948 but between 1955 and 1986 hosted the race only every other year. Which other two tracks staged the event?

4 Who is the only Formula One world champion to start more than 100 races before his first Grand Prix victory?

5 Since 2000, drivers from only four countries have won the Formula One world championship. Which countries?

6 Which Grand Prix did the legendary Brazilian driver Ayrton Senna win five times in a row between 1989 and 1993?

7 Who is the only driver to complete a Formula One season finishing on the podium in every race?

8 Ferrari engines have powered the cars of 15 Formula One world champions. Which engine supplier has been the next most successful?

9 Which Brazilian holds the record for the most career starts in Formula One but never finished higher than runner-up in the drivers' championship?

10 Which South African former Formula One world champion has a brother, Ian, who started 18 Grand Prix without gaining a single point?

11 Which British world champion was runner-up three times before landing the title?

12 What was special about Robert Kubica's victory at the 2008 Canadian Grand Prix?

13 Which unwanted record did Sebastian Vettel claim on his Formula One debut in the 2006 Turkish Grand Prix?

14 Monaco has hosted 60 Formula One Grand Prix. Only one track has staged more: which is it?

15 2013 British Grand Prix winner Nico Rosberg races under the German flag. What nationality was his father, Keke, who was world champion in 1982?

16 Italy's Ferrari team holds the record for most Formula One drivers' titles yet no Italian driver has won a Grand Prix since 2006. Name him.

17 In 2008, Lewis Hamilton became the seventh driver to be crowned world champion for McLaren. Who are the other six?

18 Which famous circuit features Casino Square, the Grand Hotel Hairpin and Piscine?

19 For which team did Michael Schumacher make his Formula One debut aged 22?

20 Before Lewis Hamilton won the 2008 drivers' title, who was the last British world champion?

Answers on page 61

09 Germany

Venue - Hockenheimring
Circuit length - 4.574km
Turns - 17

Set the unenviable task of deputising for the world-famous Nurburgring in hosting the German Grand Prix every two years, the almost totally flat Hockenheimring circuit has been shortened and given more corners, having been known as an uncomplicated, high-speed track.

The Rhine Valley venue hosted the German race every year bar one (in 1985) for 30 years until it was announced in 2006 that the event would be shared with the Nurburgring GP-Strecke.

The last champion here two years ago was Fernando Alonso, in a repeat of his 2005 and 2010 triumphs, while Britain's Lewis Hamilton is also a multiple winner, coming out on top in 2011 and his championship-winning season of 2008.

The Hockenheim event was dominated by the great Brazilians Nelson Piquet and Ayrton Senna in the late '80s, the pair sharing five race wins, while Michael Schumacher adjusted best when the track was cut from 6.8km to 4.6km in 2002, claiming victory in two of the next three races.

10 Hungary

Venue - Hungaroring, Budapest
Circuit length - 4.381km
Turns - 14 ▪ Laps - 70

The Hungaroring, 19km from the centre of Budapest, has now hosted 27 Grand Prix weekends since it became the first Formula One venue behind the Iron Curtain in 1986.

Jenson Button and Lewis Hamilton found Hungary a fertile breeding ground for British race wins. The pair have five triumphs in Budapest between them, with Button's 2006 success the first Grand Prix victory of his career.

Michael Schumacher has the most victories in Hungary – four – while Brazilian legends Ayrton Senna (3) and Nelson Piquet (2) are also multiple Budapest winners. Former World Champions Damon Hill and Fernando Alonso both secured their first race wins in Budapest, in 1993 and 2003 respectively.

Attempts were made in 2003 to remedy the narrow and twisty sections of the venue – selected only when a proposed street circuit in the middle of Budapest was deemed impractical – which made overtaking so onerous.

Schumacher is central to two of Budapest's most memorable moments. In 1997, he was passed by Hill on the last lap only for a mechanical failure to deny the Brit victory. Four years later he clinched the world title in Hungary and equalled Alain Prost's career record of 51 race wins.

DID YOU KNOW?

Triple world champion Sebastian Vettel has swept all before him in Formula One over the last few years – but is yet to win his home Grand Prix, either at the Nurburgring or in Hockenheim.

DID YOU KNOW?

The Hungarian Grand Prix was held for an astonishing 20 consecutive years in dry weather, until rain finally arrived in 2006, a factor central to Jenson Button's maiden Grand Prix win.

11 Belgium

Venue – Cir de Spa-Francorchamps, Spa
Circuit length – 7.004km
Turns – 19 ▪ **Laps** – 44

Fast, hilly and twisty, the legendary Cir de Spa-Francorchamps track in Belgium stages one of the most challenging and competitive races in the Formula One season, a favourite for many drivers.

Situated between the Belgian towns of Spa, Malmedy and Stavelot, the track was a venue during the inaugural Formula One Championship in 1950. At one stage nearly twice its current length, the circuit has retained many of its famous turns and features despite periodic safety modifications.

Eau-Rouge – a renowned 'left -right-left' sequence of corners – demands drivers climb steeply uphill flat-out before arriving at a blind summit to maximise downforce. The corner has taken on such legend, a bend at Istanbul that was likened to it was dubbed 'Faux (false) Rouge' when the Turkish Grand Prix debuted in 2005.

Cir de Spa-Francorchamps had a fearsome reputation for speed and tight corners before it was radically modified in the 1970s. Chris Bristow and Alan Stacey were killed in separate accidents in the same race in 1960, days after Stirling Moss had broken both his legs in practice.

Legends Michael Schumacher and Jim Clark boast six and four Spa wins respectively. Both also claimed the first race victories of their careers at the track, with the German's maiden triumph in 1992 denying Ayrton Senna a fifth successive win in Belgium.

DID YOU KNOW?

Cir de Spa-Francorchamps has become a staple of the F1 calendar. Despite the Belgian Grand Prix being hosted at Zolder and Nivelles between 1972 and 1982, only Monaco, Monza and Silverstone have hosted more than the 46 races staged at Spa.

12 Italy

Venue – Autodromo Nazionale Monza, Monza ▪ **Circuit length** – 5.793km
Turns – 11 ▪ **Laps** – 53

The centre of motorsport in Italy, a country so fanatical about Formula One it has become almost its heartbeat, the Autodromo Nazionale in Monza has hosted more races than any other track in the world.

The extremely quick circuit – which boasts long straights and fast corners which have been only moderately modified – hosted a weekend in F1's inaugural year of 1950, and has done so every year since apart from 1980, when Italy's Grand Prix was staged at Imola.

In appearance, the track has scarcely altered since the 1950s, and its uncompromising racing, which regrettably has also resulted in terrible accidents, is a major factor behind the reverence in which it is held in F1. The Italians are not being fanciful by referring to it as 'La Pista Magica (the magic track)'.

Ferrari have been dominant on home turf, with around twice as many race wins at Monza than any of their rivals. Five of their triumphs were earned by Michael Schumacher, the driver with the most Monza wins to his name.

Lewis Hamilton's 2012 success was the first for Britain at Monza since David Coulthard won in 1997. Strangely, the last Italian to win at Monza, in spite of the nation's motorsport fixation, was Ludovico Scarfiotti way back in 1966.

DID YOU KNOW?

The great Alberto Ascari won three times at Monza, the most of any Italian, although once was pre-F1. His father, Antonio, also triumphed there in 1924. Tragically, both perished in eerily similar circumstances while racing, each leaving a fast left-hand bend and coming to grief four days after escaping a similar crash. Both were aged 36 and survived by a wife and two children.

GP2 – Where the stars learn their trade

GP2 was the brainchild of Formula One chief Bernie Ecclestone and former Benetton F1 boss Flavio Briatore, who conceived the format as the perfect preparation for life in Formula One and it serves its purpose well.

Since it was introduced in 2005, superseding Formula 3000 as the feeder series for Formula One, around 20 per cent of drivers taking part in the GP2 series have graduated to Formula One, including the 2013 rookies Max Chilton, Esteban Gutierrez, Giedo van der Garde and Jules Bianchi.

The 2008 Formula One world champion Lewis Hamilton is GP2's star graduate – he was GP2 champion only two years earlier. Established 2013 drivers Nico Rosberg, Romain Grosjean, Nico Hulkenberg and Pastor Maldonado are also former GP2 champions.

All teams in GP2 must use the same chassis, engine and tyres so that true driver ability is reflected. Two GP2 races – one of 180 kilometres and a 'sprint' event over 120km – are staged as support events at F1 weekends so that drivers can also experience the Grand Prix environment.

Here are four GP2 drivers hoping to be among the next to make the step up:

Sam Bird
(Great Britain)

Surrey-based Sam Bird worked his way up through Formula BMW, Formula Renault and Formula Three before making his GP2 debut for ART Grand Prix in 2009-10 at the GP2 Asia series before scoring his first win at the Monza feature race to finish fifth in GP2 2010.

Switching to iSport International in 2011, he was joint top of the standings after four races before his commitments as a Formula One test driver for Mercedes took priority.

After a year away, when he had to fit competitive racing in the World Series by Renault around his commitments with Mercedes, Bird returned to GP2 in 2013 with the Russian Time team and won races in Bahrain and Monaco before scoring an impressive success at Silverstone on British Grand Prix weekend.

Jon Lancaster
(Great Britain)

Leeds-born Jon Lancaster enjoyed success in Formula Renault and Formula Three as a teenager but it was his success at the British Grand Prix meeting at Silverstone last year that brought him to wider notice, justifying the Hilmer team's decision to pair him with highly-rated Sauber test driver Robin Frijns in their 2013 GP2 line-up.

Lancaster held off the Indonesian driver Rio Haryanto and Britain's highly-rated James Calado to win the GP2 sprint race and give Britain a weekend GP2 double following Sam Bird's victory in the longer race, where Lancaster was also among the points, finishing fifth.

Without the financial support enjoyed by some of his rival drivers, Lancaster has had to work hard to make himself noticed but proved the Silverstone win was no fluke by winning the German GP2 sprint event at the Nurburgring the following weekend.

Stefano Coletti
(Monaco)

The first Monaco-born driver since Louis Chiron in 1931 to win a race on home soil, Coletti achieved that distinction when he took the sprint event at the principality's race weekend in May 2013, when he enjoyed the best of his four seasons so far in GP2.

Coletti, who had switched from Scuderia Coloni to Rapax midway through a 2012 campaign in which he finished a disappointing 13th, continued the association on 2013 with great success, winning the sprint races in Malaysia and Spain as well as Monaco.

A points scorer in six other early races for the Italy-based team – formerly Minardi Piquet Sports – Coletti was bidding to emulate Pastor Maldonado's 2010 GP2 title triumph for Rapax.

Felipe Nasr
(Brazil)

Seen by many judges as a driver likely to follow in Brazil's rich tradition of success in Formula One, Nasr is a former European Formula Renault champion and British Formula Three champion who placed as second best rookie when he raced alongside eventual champion Davide Valsecchi in the 2012 GP2 season while still only 19.

For 2013, Nasr returned to Carlin, for whom he had won the British F3 title in 2011 with an impressive seven race wins and 17 podium finishes in 30 races.

Promising to give the likes of James Calado and Sam Bird a run for their money, Nasr impressed with his consistency and was rarely outside the points. Formula One bosses were watching his progress carefully and has been tipped to make a breakthrough in 2014.

MAX CHILTON

Son of the multi-millionaire Carlin Motorsport owner Grahame Chilton and brother of touring car driver Tom, Max Chilton grew up immersed in racing and surprised few people by completing the journey to the Formula One grid last year.

Chilton, who was privately educated at Ardingly College, joined Marussia midway through the 2012 season as a test driver. His early F1 experiences have centred on the Yas Marina Circuit in Abu Dhabi; he took part in his first practice session there with Marussia in 2012 and, the year before, drove for Force India in a Young Driver test.

His achievements at such a young age are as good a sign as any that Chilton could achieve great things in motorsport with the right application. Turning 23 this year, Chilton graduated from karting to British Formula Three in 2007, despite having been below the required age of 16 when the season began.

He has driven for his father's Carlin team in various disciplines and partnered brother Tom – who has regularly appeared on BBC motoring show Top Gear – in the 2007 1000km of Silverstone. From 2010, he raced in the GP2 series for three full seasons, finishing fourth after two race wins in 2012.

Chilton could have been forgiven for being daunted by the prospect of following experienced German Timo Glock. But the ambitious Anglo-Russian team have a commitment to nurturing young talent and Chilton has responded to this positive atmosphere.

FACT PANEL

BORN: April 21, 1991; Reigate, England
2013 TEAM: Marussia
DEBUT: 2013 Australian GP (Marussia)
BEST FORMULA ONE RACE: 16th in 2013 Malaysian GP (Marussia)
BEST GP2 SERIES SEASON: 4th in 2009 (Marussia Carlin)

GIEDO VAN DER GARDE

Dutchman Giedo van der Garde looked to have missed his chance in Formula One after spells as reserve driver with Super Aguri and Spyker had not provided him the platform to make the final leap to a race seat.

After five years away he was handed another reserve driver opportunity in 2012, this time with Caterham. The Malaysian-owned team took the surprising decision to sever ties with Heikki Kovalainen and Vitaly Petrov in the winter, opening the door for rookie 26-year-old Van der Garde to take a permanent spot on the grid for the first time.

McLaren offered the Dutchman a berth on their coveted Young Drivers Programme in 2006 but after ultimately leaving Spyker following a contract dispute, Van der Garde was forced to restore his reputation in other disciplines.

He scooped his sole title in the Formula Renault 3.5 series in 2008, winning five races and reaching eight podiums for P1 Motorsport that year. He also competed in four GP2 seasons, including in 2012 as part of his Formula One contract with Caterham, for whom he won two races en route to a sixth-place finish. Van der Garde is no stranger to competing with the best either; in 2006 he finished sixth in Formula Three Euro Series in 2006 behind Sebastian Vettel and Paul Di Resta.

FACT PANEL

BORN: April 25, 1985; Rhenen, Netherlands
2013 TEAM: Caterham
DEBUT: 2013 Australian GP (Caterham)
BEST FORMULA ONE RACE: 15th in 2013 Malaysian GP (Caterham)
BEST FORMULA RENAULT 3.5 SEASON: 1st in 2008 (P1 Motorsport)

HEIKKI KOVALAINEN

In being retained by Caterham as a test driver for 2013, Heikki Kovalainen showed he still has the hunger and aptitude to compete in the upper echelons of Formula One.

It was a surprise when the former McLaren driver and Vitaly Petrov were replaced by Caterham in 2011, Kovalainen having been praised for the team's steady development, but the Finn's fine record in F1 surely ensures his future remains at the top of motorsport. A product of the Renault driver development programme, Kovalainen had beaten Michael Schumacher and David Coulthard to win the 2004 Race of Champions but was forced to wait until 2007 for a race seat in F1.

In that maiden year, Kovalainen finished second in Japan and finished seventh in the drivers' standings, attracting the advances of McLaren, who recruited him as teammate to Lewis Hamilton. He claimed his first and – to date – sole race victory in Hungary for the British-based team in 2008, but was forced to make way for world champion Jenson Button at the end of the 2009 season.

Kovalainen took to racing at the age of 10 before making a name for himself in karting and winning the 'Rookie of the Year' award for winning two races in his debut season in the 2001 British Formula Renault season. He also won five times in his first season in Formula Three to finish 3rd and scooped his first title in 2004 by winning the World Series by Nissan.

FACT PANEL

BORN: October 19, 1981; Suomussalmi, Finland
2013 TEAM: Caterham (test driver)
DEBUT: 2007 Australian GP (Renault)
FIRST FORMULA ONE WIN: 2008 Hungarian GP (McLaren)
BEST F1 SEASON: 7th in 2007 (Renault) and 2008 (McLaren)

ROBERT KUBICA

No one would be more deserving of a World Championship than Robert Kubica if the Pole was able to return to Formula One after an extended absence from the sport following serious injury.

After an encouraging 2010 season with new team Renault, Kubica was lucky to escape with his life after crashing during the first stage of the Ronde di Andora rally. Suffering such major injuries as a partially amputated arm and fractures to his elbow, shoulder and leg, Kubica survived the crash and the seven-hour wait to be extricated from his car, but was unable to race in Formula One in 2011 and 2012. Last year, the unperturbed former BMW Sauber driver returned to regular competitive racing with Citroen in the European and World Rally-2 Championships.

Kubica was hotly-tipped as a future champion in his childhood karting days but had big shoes to fill when he was handed his first Formula One chance aged 21. BMW Sauber called in test driver Kubica for the 2006 Hungarian Grand Prix after former world champion Jacques Villeneuve was deemed unfit.

Shortly after, the Canadian left BMW Sauber, paving the way for Kubica to join permanently. He claimed his only race victory to date in Canada in 2008, one of 12 podium finishes in his career. In reaching podiums at Monaco, Spa-Francorchamps and Interlagos – tracks renowned for rewarding driver prowess over engineering excellence – Kubica has left nobody doubting the extent of his natural talent.

FACT PANEL

BORN: December 7, 1984; Krakow, Poland
2013 TEAM: Citroen (European and World Rally-2 Championships)
DEBUT: 2006 Hungarian GP (BMW Sauber)
FIRST F1 RACE WIN: 2008 Canadian GP (BMW Sauber)
BEST F1 SEASON: 4th in 2008 (BMW Sauber)

Facts and Stats

Britain's 2008 world champion Lewis Hamilton has not always confined his speed to the track – in 2007 he was banned from driving in France for a month after being clocked at 122mph in an 85mph-limit on a French motorway.

Alain Prost won his home Grand Prix on four different tracks in France – Dijon, the Paul Ricard Full Circuit, the Paul Ricard Short Circuit and Magny-Cours.

Formula One boss Bernie Ecclestone held a secret ambition to drive in a Grand Prix when he bought the Connaught-Alta team in 1958 but after failing in his attempt to qualify for the Monaco race the same year vowed to stick to management.

The first British driver to win a Grand Prix was Mike Hawthorn, who won for Ferrari at Reims in France in July 1953.

Ferrari is the only team to have contested every season of Formula One since its inception in 1950.

Britain's Nigel Mansell claimed sixth place in the 1984 Dallas Grand Prix by pushing his Lotus across the finish line after his gearbox failed.

In 2012 Bernie Ecclestone offered to stump up £35 million from his own fortune to stage a London Grand Prix on a route that would see racing cars pass Buckingham Palace and the Houses of Parliament at speeds of up to 180mph.

The late Gilles Villeneuve and his son Jacques are the only two out of 15 Canadian drivers in the history of Formula One to have won points.

The British racing team Arrows competed in 368 Grands Prix between 1978 and 2002 but its notoriously unreliable cars failed to win a single race. In the 1987 Hungarian GP, Damon Hill led by 35 seconds only to be passed on the last lap after suffering a hydraulic failure.

In 1988, McLaren drivers Ayrton Senna and Alain Prost won 15 of the season's 16 Grands Prix, including a record 11 consecutively. Their only failure came at Monza, when both retired and Gerhard Berger scored a home victory for Ferrari.

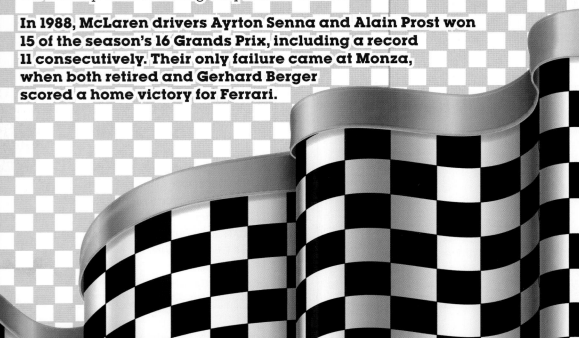

13 Singapore

Venue - Marina Bay Street Circuit, Singapore
Circuit length - 5.073km
Turns - 23 ▪ Laps - 61

The first Grand Prix in Formula One history to be staged at night, the Singapore race at the Marina Bay Street Circuit has overcome initial scepticism to be a huge success.

From its debut weekend in 2008, the city-state's famous and spectacular skyline has provided a stunning, illuminated backdrop for victories for Fernando Alonso, Lewis Hamilton and Sebastian Vettel.

The event's timing makes it convenient for European TV audiences and the partly street circuit replicates daylight conditions for drivers using powerful lighting systems. Less accommodating for drivers is the prevailing heat and humidity in Singapore which, together with regular bumps and kerbs, exerts great physical pressure on participants.

Modifications had to be made in the wake of Marina Bay's 2008 bow, such as turn alterations to make overtaking easier, and the success of the Singapore race has so far had no detrimental impact on the Grand Prix in nearby Malaysia, something organisers at Sepang feared initially.

A vision of the Singapore government for the race to form part of a national festival has come true; in 2010 the race formed part of a 10-day entertainment schedule which included parties, concerts and exhibitions.

DID YOU KNOW?

The Singapore Grand Prix may have arrived in Formula One only in 2008, but it also was staged as a day-time Formula Libre race between 1966 and 1973 at a circuit called Thomson Road.

14 South Korea

Venue - Korea International Circuit, Yeongam
Circuit length - 5.615km
Turns - 18 ▪ Laps - 55

After hosting the 1988 Olympics and 2002 World Cup, there was no surprise at South Korea's ambition to add a Formula One Grand Prix to its illustrious list of sporting events staged.

By using a stunning waterside location for the Korea International Circuit, the country realised that aim in 2010, finishing the track just days before its inaugural race.

Echoing the ventures made into F1 by near neighbours China and Singapore, Korea certainly hit the right notes with the part-permanent, part-temporary track in the South Jeolla region. Featuring an enormous 1.2km straight and several slow and fast turns, it should retain its place in the competitive F1 calendar until at least 2021.

The largely rural venue is 400km from Seoul but the new track is expected to stimulate growth for the city of Jeollanam-do, with plans for business parks and entertainment complexes in the pipeline.

Sebastian Vettel's 2011 triumph sealed the Constructors' Championship for Red Bull with three races to spare, 24 hours after Lewis Hamilton had broken Red Bull's incredible streak of 15 consecutive pole positions.

DID YOU KNOW?

In the first three races staged at Yeongam, the driver who claimed pole position failed to win the race. Twice winner Sebastian Vettel qualified first in 2010 when Fernando Alonso ultimately won the race.

15 India

Venue - Buddh International Circuit, Uttar Pradesh
Circuit length - 5.125km
Turns - 16 ▪ Laps - 60

The arrival of Formula One to a suburb of New Delhi was the culmination of sustained efforts to bring the sport to India, with locations in Mumbai and Hyderabad considered as early as 2004.

The Buddh Circuit in Noida, which has, through its two sizeable straights and interesting mix of bends, attracted praise and comparisons to the legendary Spa-Francorchamps in Belgium, finally fulfilled the Indian dream in 2011.

The splash of colour and glamour of Bollywood is always evident at the event, which in its maiden year coincided with the Diwali festival, further increasing visitor figures and consumer spending.

Red Bull's Sebastian Vettel made the new circuit his own in 2011 and 2012, winning in Buddh en route to successive World Championships. His victories from Jenson Button and Fernando Alonso respectively were extremely comfortable.

After Sachin Tendulkar fulfilled the role in 2011, the Indian organisers continued to bestow the honour of waving the chequered flag on their successful sportspeople. Shooter Gagan Narang, who scooped a bronze medal at the London Olympics, did the honours in 2012.

DID YOU KNOW?

The track is part of a 2,500 acre sports park called the Jaypee Greens Sports City. Also planned for the park is a 100,000-seater cricket stadium, a 25,000-seater hockey ground and an 18-hole golf course.

16 Abu Dhabi

Venue - Yas Marina Circuit
Circuit length - 5.554km
Turns - 21
Laps - 55

A manifestation of the rewards reaped from huge oil reserves, Formula One racing in the wealthy city of Abu Dhabi has been the commercial and glamour success many people envisaged when it debuted in 2009.

The host of another day-night weekend, the beautifully-located Yas Marina circuit twists a path around the sophisticated marina of Yas Island.

This track with a stunning backdrop is no mere improvised street circuit and has provided high-quality racing already in its short life in F1. The longest straight on the F1 calendar contributes to high speed sections while slow and precise turns provide frequent overtaking opportunities.

The first two Abu Dhabi races were afforded the prestigious final spot in the calendar, and Sebastian Vettel secured his maiden World Championship at Yas Marina in 2010, 12 months after he also won the inaugural Grand Prix there.

Kimi Raikkonen's triumph in 2012 was doubly special; it was the 2007 World Champion's first since returning to Formula One and handed the famous name of Lotus a first victory since they resumed racing.

DID YOU KNOW?

Two years before Abu Dhabi first hosted a race, Formula One came to the area in the form of a festival. The event was the first of its kind and the largest gathering of F1 constructors and drivers outside of a race. The agreement to stage races in Abu Dhabi from 2009 was made just days later.

25 Years Ago – 1989

By 1989, the Frenchman Alain Prost had already established himself as one of Formula One's greats – the first French world champion in 1985, the first back-to-back champion for 26 years when he retained the title in 1986 and in 1987 the most successful driver of all time (before Michael Schumacher came on the scene) when he overtook Jackie Stewart's 14-year-old record of 27 race victories.

But the driver known as 'the Professor' for his carefully thought-out strategies also had a history of conflict, having broken his first contract with McLaren only to then fall out with Renault and go back to McLaren. Yet nothing was to match the feud that developed between him and Ayrton Senna after the Brazilian became his teammate in 1988.

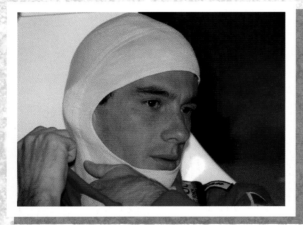

Senna won the title in 1988, scoring eight race wins to Prost's seven and several incidents on the track began to sour their relationship, with Prost accusing his teammate of dangerous driving and resenting his public popularity.

As the 1989 season unfolded, their mutual admiration had become mutual hatred, the pair barely speaking to each other for six months. Matters came to a head in the penultimate race, the Japanese GP at Suzuka, which Senna needed to win to stay in contention.

Senna tried to pass Prost at the chicane before the start-finish straight on lap 46 of the 53 but Prost blocked his move and the two skidded into the escape road and stalled. Prost, who had a big lead in the title race, climbed out of his car but Senna got a push start from marshals, pitted for repairs and rejoined the race, overtaking Alessandro Nannini's Benetton to finish first.

Prost, having seen Senna rejoin the race, stormed into the race marshals' office to complain and the Brazilian was disqualified for cutting the chicane. The matter went to court, but Senna's appeal was lost and Prost confirmed as champion.

Kimi Raikkonen

One of the most relaxed and popular competitors in Formula One, 2007 World Champion Kimi Raikkonen 's return to the sport with Lotus has been a major success story.

The Finn, known as 'The Iceman' for being so calm that he regularly sleeps before races, quit F1 in 2009 to compete in three seasons of the world rally championship, just two years after he won the world championship with Ferrari. He also tried his hand at NASCAR and was heavily linked with Renault when he left the Italian giants.

Lured back to F1 to drive under the iconic name of Lotus, Raikkonen underlined his incredible ability by

finishing third in the standings in 2012, beating both McLarens, Felipe Massa's Ferrari and Mark Webber of Red Bull in the process.

It was this natural talent that secured him a berth in Formula One originally, aged only 21, after just one season working for Sauber as a test driver. After driving with pace and consistency throughout the season, the UK Formula Renault champion of 2000 had alerted several potential suitors.

McLaren soon earmarked him as a successor to two-times champion, Mika Hakkinen, the original 'flying Finn'. There were fears Raikkonen might find this a step too far, given his inexperience, but he silenced the sceptics, claiming a maiden race win in Malaysia in 2003. He reached 10 further podiums that year to finish second in the drivers' championship, only two points behind Michael Schumacher.

With McLaren, he was runner-up again in 2005, scooping seven race wins only to lose out unluckily to the Renault of Fernando Alonso. He was less competitive in 2006, but was given the ultimate compliment in 2007 when Ferrari chose him to replace the legendary Schumacher.

Raikkonen dealt with the pressure comfortably, winning on his team debut in Australia before triumphing in France, Britain, Belgium and China before regaining the lead in the final race in Brazil. By a quirk, his final points tally of 110 in his title-winning season was two fewer than his total for McLaren in 2005 when he finished only second.

FACT PANEL

BORN: October 17, 1979; Espoo, Finland
2013 TEAM: Lotus
DEBUT: 2001 Australian GP (Sauber)
FIRST F1 WIN: 2003 Malaysian (McLaren)
FIRST F1 TITLE: 2007 (Ferrari)

Silverstone

Ten things you might not know about Silverstone,
the home of British motor racing.

1 The circuit was built on the site of RAF Silverstone in Northamptonshire, a World War II bomber station. It incorporated two of the runways.

2 It became home to the British Grand Prix, although the race was originally staged at the Brooklands circuit, in Surrey.

3 The first organised race staged there was the RAC International Grand Prix in October 1948. It was won by the Italian driver, Luigi Villoresi, in a Maserati.

4 Silverstone hosted the first event of the very first Formula One Grand Prix season in 1950, won by another Italian, Giuseppe Farina, in a Ferrari. It was watched by a crowd of 100,000.

5 The inaugural Formula One race was attended by King George VI and Queen Elizabeth, the first and only time a reigning monarch has been present at a motor race in Britain.

6 In 1977, Silverstone became home to the British Motorcycle Grand Prix, replacing the Isle of Man TT as the British leg of the world championship after the latter was deemed to be too dangerous for international competition.

7 Of the 10 British drivers who have been Formula One world champions, three – Mike Hawthorn, Graham Hill and John Surtees – ended their careers without winning a British Grand Prix at Silverstone. Jenson Button has yet to finish higher than fourth in 14 attempts.

8 Silverstone's Club Corner was named in honour of the original Royal Automobile Club in Pall Mall, London. The Woodcote Corner takes its name from the stately home in Surrey bought by the RAC in 1913 for use by its members.

9 The fastest lap recorded at Silverstone was set by the Finnish driver Keke Rosberg in practice for the 1985 British Grand Prix, with an average speed of 160.9mph. Until Juan Pablo Montoya lapped the Monza circuit at 161.5mph in 2002 it was the fastest lap in Formula One history.

10 When Peter Collins became the first British driver to win at Silverstone in 1958, 12 of the 20 cars in competition were driven by British drivers, including the first four to cross the finish line.

20 Years Ago - 1994

The 1994 Formula One season featured Michael Schumacher's maiden drivers' title – won by a single point from Damon Hill – but was completely overshadowed by the death of the triple world champion Ayrton Senna.

Senna was in only his third race for Williams when the fatal accident happened at the San Marino GP at Imola. He had left McLaren after three titles in four years to replace his bitter rival, the defending champion, Alain Prost, who had announced his retirement.

Chillingly, Senna had warned before the season began that changes to the cars to reduce the reliance on technology would lead to "a lot of accidents." His own came at the Tamburello corner on the seventh lap, when he lost control and hit an unprotected wall at 131mph, causing a wheel to break away, hitting him on the head. He was airlifted to hospital but could not be saved. In a poignant postscript, an Austrian flag was found in Senna's cockpit; had he won the race, he had intended to wave it in memory of Austrian rookie driver Roland Ratzenberger, killed when he lost control of his car in practice, also hitting a wall at speed.

Schumacher finished the race first but there were no celebrations on the podium. The German won the first four races of the season and six of the first seven in the Benetton-Ford but Hill, who interrupted the sequence by winning in Spain, took five of the next eight in the Williams-Renault to Schumacher's two.

Going into the final race, the Australian GP, Schumacher led Hill by a single point but after going off the track and damaging his own car he controversially collided with Hill on lap 35 as the latter tried to overtake. Both cars were eliminated and, as neither driver scored, Schumacher took the title.

17 USA – Texas

Venue – Circuit of the Americas, Austin, Texas

Circuit length – 5.513km

Turns – 20 ▪ Laps – 56

The United States was conspicuous by its absence between 2007 and 2012 but now boasts two precious Formula One weekends, with the Circuit of the Americas in Texas having led the country's return to the sport two years ago.

Lewis Hamilton provided interesting symmetry on the US Grand Prix's return – his victory at the new track in 2012's penultimate race came five years after he triumphed in the final race held at the Indianapolis Speedway.

Hermann Tilke's circuit takes advantage of natural inclines to include elevation changes of up to 40m. Turn One – a steep uphill straight into a hairpin turn – is the stand out feature.

Texan races can be watched by more than 120,000 fans, owing to grandstands, temporary structures and natural seating areas, while the site also houses a medical facility, meeting suites, conference facilities and banquet halls.

Austin's F1 involvement dates back only recently but the US Grand Prix was first staged in Formula One in 1959 and has been held in California, Florida, New York, Arizona and, finally, at Indianapolis. Michael Schumacher has the most US Grand Prix victories at any venue with five.

18 USA – New Jersey

Venue – Port Imperial Street Circuit, New Jersey

Circuit length – 5.2km

Turns – 19 ▪ Laps – 59

Blessed with arguably Formula One's most stunning backdrop, the new Port Imperial Street Circuit in New Jersey will add further glitz and glamour to motorsport when it hosts its first Grand Prix in 2014.

Just across the Hudson River from the towering Manhattan skyline, New Jersey was originally set to debut in F1 last year but had to be put back after construction delays.

The location of the track – yet another Hermann Tilke-inspired circuit – was chosen for its stunning elevation changes of up to 47m and excellent access to public transportation.

Like the famous Monaco track, the New Jersey facility will take in residential areas, as well one of its longer straights running along the waterfront of the Hudson.

The introduction of the Grand Prix of America is not the first time organisers have tried to bring F1 to the New York area; a race was announced for the 1983 season only to be cancelled when one of the preferred venues – the Meadowlands Sports Complex – opted to stage an Indy 500 race instead.

DID YOU KNOW?

The keenness of organisers to attract Formula One to the United States is clear but the sport is some way from the level of support enjoyed across the Atlantic by Nascar and the IndyCar series. No American has won their country's Grand Prix in Formula One format, while the last American to win an F1 race anywhere was Mario Andretti way back in 1978.

DID YOU KNOW?

The failure to ready the New Jersey circuit for a Grand Prix last year meant the 2013 F1 calendar had to be cut to 19 races – Istanbul's weekend had already been axed from the schedule to make way.

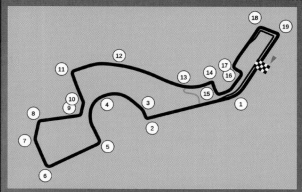

19 Brazil

Venue – Interlagos, Sao Paulo

Circuit length – 4.309km

Turns – 15 ▪ Laps – 71

Having established itself as the final destination of the Formula One calendar, the character-filled Interlagos track in Sao Paulo remains one of the sport's most exciting despite radical 1980s alterations.

Interlagos was eight kilometres long, almost double its current length, when it first staged F1 racing in 1973, with home favourite Emerson Fittipaldi claiming victory that year.

Safety concerns relating to bumpy sections, inadequate barriers and deep ditches meant Interlagos lost the Brazilian Grand Prix for ten years, finally reclaiming it in 1990 after shortening the circuit and carrying out extensive redevelopment.

Sebastian Vettel sealed his third straight Drivers' Championship at Interlagos last year, joining a long list of winners to be crowned in Brazil. A particularly thrilling recent example was in 2008, when Lewis Hamilton's denied Felipe Massa – the race winner – by overtaking Timo Glock after his Brazilian rival had completed the race.

Nine Brazilians have finished first at their own Grand Prix, although Nelson Piquet's brace of victories were in Rio rather than at Interlagos. The track is officially named after one of the Brazilian Interlagos victors, Carlos Pace, whose career was cut short by a plane crash in 1977.

DID YOU KNOW?

Treacherous weather at Interlagos in 2003 caused many leading drivers to spin off, including World Champion Michael Schumacher. It ended a remarkable sequence of finishing races which dated back two years. Giancarlo Fisichella's eventual win was the maiden Grand Prix triumph of his career.

20 Russia

Venue – Sochi International Street Circuit, Sochi

Circuit length – 5.872km

Turns – 19

The Sochi International Street Circuit is set to end years of suggestions and deliberations by finally bringing Formula One racing to Russia over the coming years.

There were sustained attempts to host a race in the old Soviet Union, with a proposed Grand Prix in Moscow included on the provisional calendar for 1983 only to be thwarted by bureaucratic barriers.

Bernie Ecclestone ultimately succeeded in organising a race behind the Iron Curtain, with Hungary awarded a race soon after, and Russia was forced to consider new locations after the Berlin Wall fell.

Russian President Vladimir Putin strongly advocated a circuit near Pulkovo Airport in St Petersburg in 2001, while a development called Nagatino Island in northern Moscow was suggested in 2003, but both never came to fruition.

A spot on the provisional F1 2014 calendar was awarded to Russia after they proposed to stage a weekend in the Black Sea resort of Sochi, on the same site as venues for the 2014 Winter Olympics.

DID YOU KNOW?

If the move to Sochi is successful for F1 the Russian Grand Prix will be staged for the first time in 100 years. The race has been staged only twice before, with Russian Georgy Suvorin winning the last one 1914

The team behind the champion - the story of Red Bull

Thanks to the brilliance behind the wheel of Sebastian Vettel, the Red Bull name is as familiar to Formula One fans as Ferrari or McLaren – yet until 2005 the Red Bull team did not exist. Its meteoric rise from newcomer to double world champions in five years shows just what can be achieved by the right people with the right support.

Amazingly, the racing team that formed the starting point for Red Bull was bought for just one US dollar, the nominal purchase price the Ford Motor Company set when it decided to offload the unsuccessful Jaguar Formula One team, provided that whoever bought it committed 400 million US dollars to investing in the team.

The buyer was Dietrich Mateschitz, the Austrian businessman who founded Red Bull energy drinks. Mateschitz, a sports fanatic, already owned the successful football clubs Red Bull Salzburg and Red Bull New York and had been involved with motor racing through the company's sponsorship of the Swiss F1 team Sauber.

Mateschitz aims high for his new Milton Keynes-based team, hiring the former Williams and McLaren driver David Coulthard as lead driver and the successful Arden Formula 3000 boss Christian Horner as team director. The first two races yields more points than the team had managed all season in its last year as Jaguar F1.

Then comes Mateschitz's next bold move, tempting the brilliant British designer Adrian Newey – whose cars had won six world titles for Williams and McLaren in the 1990s – to quit McLaren for Red Bull in 2006.

Coulthard gives the team its first podium finish when he comes home third at Monaco in 2006 and Mark Webber is announced as Red Bull's latest driving recruit. Coulthard finishes 10th in the 2007 driver standings but 2008 is disappointing – Webber achieves a run of points finishes but in the constructors' championship Red Bull are outperformed even by Toro Rosso, its Italian-based supposedly junior team.

But a corner is turned with Newey's RB5 car in 2009. With Vettel moving across from Toro Rosso after his stunning maiden F1 victory at the Italian GP, Red Bull scores a one-two in Shanghai and another at Silverstone. Webber wins in Germany and Brazil, Vettel in Japan and Abu Dhabi. Vettel finishes runner-up to Jenson Button in the drivers' championship and the team comes second behind Brawn in the constructors' chart.

The RB6 is better still, bringing Red Bull 15 pole positions in 19 races in 2010, which result in nine

victories and both championships. Vettel wins five races to Webber's four. Newey is the first designer to win Formula One titles with three different teams

Vettel takes charge in 2011, driving Newey's RB7 to 11 victories and six other podium finishes, only twice finishing outside the first three, and takes a third title in a row in the RB8 in 2012 after Newey irons out some early season problems, a late-season surge carrying him past Ferrari's Fernando Alonso to win by a mere three points. Red Bull completes a hat-trick of constructors' championships, too, leaving Mateschitz to reflect that he had never spent a dollar more wisely.

PASTOR MALDONADO

Pastor Maldonado rewrote history by becoming the first Venezuelan to win a Grand Prix when he triumphed at Barcelona in 2012. Hopes this would catapult him into the group of drivers regularly fighting for championship points proved slightly premature, however.

Maldonado, who has driven for Williams for the last three seasons, won four regional and three national karting championships before reaching 14. Moving to Europe, he won the Italian Formula Renault series in 2004, winning eight races en route, and came eighth in the fiercely competitive European Formula Renault V.6 series the same year.

After first testing in F1 for Minardi, his 2005 was frustrating but he finished 3rd in the 2006 Formula Renault 3.5 series, which secured him a seat in GP2 for 2007 with Trident. He won impressively in Monaco in only his fifth race and finished the season in 11th despite missing four races with a fractured collarbone.

Maldonado hoped for an F1 seat in 2010 after fifth and sixth finishes in GP2 with ART but he turned his misfortune into a very successful season. Winning six races for Rapax, he stormed to the 2010 GP2 title by a crushing 16-point margin, enough evidence to persuade Williams to offer him their second race seat for 2011.

He picked up only one point from his debut season but with a much improved Renault-powered car he scored his first victory from pole at the 2012 Spanish GP, giving Williams their first race win for eight years. More victories have not been readily forthcoming since with any championship points a scarcity for Williams last season.

FACT PANEL

BORN: March 10, 1985; Maracay, Venezuela
2013 TEAM: Williams
DEBUT: 2011 Australian GP (Williams)
FIRST F1 WIN: 2012 Spanish GP (Williams)
BEST F1 SEASON: 19th in 2011 (Williams)

PAUL DI RESTA

Paul di Resta follows greats such as Jackie Stewart, Jim Clark and David Coulthard in providing a Scottish presence in Formula One, with his team Force India finally showing the pace necessary to compete for points.

Of Italian heritage, Di Resta matched his paltry 2011 points tally of 27 in just eight races in 2012, highlighting his steady progress. Cousin of Scottish-born Indycar champion Dario Franchitti, he was tipped as a future talent by McLaren in 2004, when they named him their Autosport BRDC Young Driver of the Year after he finished 3rd in the UK Formula Renault.

He claimed the 2006 Formula Three Euro Series crown with ASM, winning five times against a field that included future F1 world champion Sebastian Vettel. Backed by Mercedes-Benz, Di Resta spent four seasons in the ultra-competitive DTM touring car championship in Germany, where he finished 5th, 2nd and 3rd before beating off competition from fellow-Scot Coulthard and Ralf Schumacher to win the title with HWA in 2010.

Meanwhile he was posting excellent times in F1 testing with Force India. His nomination as 'Rookie of the Year' was inevitable after finishing 13th in the drivers' championship in his first year in 2011. In Bahrain in 2013 he was denied a maiden podium finish by Lotus' Romain Grosjean but did beat Lewis Hamilton, Mark Webber and Fernando Alonso to finish 4th.

FACT PANEL

BORN: April 16, 1986; Uphall, Scotland
2013 TEAM: Force India
DEBUT: 2011 Australian GP (Force India)
BEST F1 RACE: 4th in 2012 Singapore GP and 2013 Bahrain GP (both Force India)
BEST F1 SEASON: 13th in 2011 (Force India)

NICO HULKENBERG

Yet another member of a German generation inspired by the astonishing successes of Michael Schumacher, Nico Hulkenberg has links with the Ferrari great that are even more tangible than that.

In winning the 2003 German karting championship Hulkenberg was emulating Schumacher's efforts 16 years previously. With Schumacher's manager Willi Weber looking after his affairs, he then made a spectacular step up to German Formula BMW in 2005 – aged 18 – by comfortably winning the title with eight wins, replicating the achievement of another German high-flyer, Sebastian Vettel.

In 2008, he was invited by Williams to test in F1 for them, an arrangement that turned into a permanent deal. He combined that work with an F3 Euroseries title in 2008, secured with seven race wins. A year on he raced in GP2, where again he excelled, winning five times to be champion with a race to spare.

His F1 breakthrough came with Williams in 2010 but even though he was 10th in Malaysia and 6th in Hungary, he was dropped for 2011 in favour of Pastor Maldonado.

A switch to Force India as test driver in 2011 turned into a position on the grid in 2012. Hulkenberg went on to have an unexpectedly successful season in 2012, regularly registering points and sealing his best race result at Spa-Francorchamps.

FACT PANEL

BORN: August 19, 1987; Emmerich am Rhein, Germany
2013 TEAM: Sauber
DEBUT: 2010 Australian GP (Williams)
BEST F1 RACE: 4th in 2012 Belgian GP (Force India)
BEST F1 SEASON: 11th in 2012 (Force India)

CHARLES PIC

After shining alongside a more experienced teammate in Timo Glock at Marussia, Charles Pic has been forced to remain content at fighting for positions at the back of the grid since moving to Caterham last year.

The Frenchman was steered into motor racing by his godfather – former F1 driver Eric Barnard – who bought him a kart before he was 12. After making impressive progress in junior categories, he raced in the French Formula Campus championship at the tender age of 16 and created an immediate impression by finishing 3rd after two wins, before finishing 3rd again in the Formula Renault 2.0 Eurocup in 2007.

In two seasons in the Renault Formula 3.5 Series he finished 6th and 3rd, finding time in 2009 to debut in GP2 and record his first win, for Arden in the Asia Series. He stepped up to the main GP2 series in 2010, again with Arden, winning one race before finishing 4th overall after notching up wins in Spain and Monaco.

Invited by Virgin to practise in F1, he performed well at the young driver test in Abu Dhabi in November 2011 and was signed to replace Jerome D'Ambrosio in their 2012 line-up. He made a creditable start that promised greater things once he has the chance to drive a more competitive car. So far at Caterham, partnering inexperienced Dutchman Giedo van der Garde, he has remained some way from scoring points.

FACT PANEL

BORN: February 15, 1990; Montelimar, France
2013 TEAM: Caterham
DEBUT: 2012 Australian GP (Marussia)
BEST F1 RACE: 12th in 2012 Brazilian GP (Marussia)
BEST F1 SEASON: 21st in 2012 (Marussia)

Page 30 - Champions Wordsearch

M	A	G	N	O	E	Y	S	Z	M	B	T	L	G
A	K	N	A	W	N	H	K	I	X	T	G	Z	R
K	T	S	F	P	A	X	E	K	E	H	R	F	O
U	S	B	A	N	S	H	M	A	N	S	E	C	K
Z	P	I	G	K	N	M	U	T	R	I	A	T	U
U	V	H	L	E	H	S	Z	N	U	N	T	J	A
S	A	Z	K	V	T	I	T	W	O	G	E	R	L
I	F	C	H	I	E	M	R	M	B	A	R	M	A
J	O	X	N	R	R	R	D	V	L	P	N	X	L
H	B	U	D	A	P	E	S	T	E	O	O	A	U
I	B	A	H	D	U	B	A	T	M	R	I	Z	M
J	T	S	A	O	P	A	U	L	O	E	D	N	P
L	Z	D	Y	N	K	N	K	Z	Y	N	A	O	U
L	A	E	R	T	N	O	M	T	H	Y	E	M	R

Page 34 – Twenty Questions

1) Britain's Lewis Hamilton won the race, beating Vettel by less than a second.

2) Four -- Canada, United States, Hungary and Japan.

3) Aintree in Liverpool, and then Brands Hatch in Kent.

4) Britain's 2009 champion Jenson Button, who did not win a Grand Prix until the 2006 Hungarian GP, his 113th start.

5) Germany (Michael Schumacher, Sebastian Vettel), Great Britain (Lewis Hamilton, Jenson Button), Spain (Fernando Alonso) and Finland (Kimi Räikkönen)

6) Monaco, where he won a record six times in total.

7) Michael Schumacher, who finished in the first two in 16 from 17 races in 2002, winning 11 races. He was third in the Malaysian GP.

8) Ford, who supplied engines for 12 champions between 1968 and 1982 and powered Michael Schumacher's Benetton in 1994.

9) Rubens Barrichello, who started 322 races between 1993 and 2011 and was twice runner-up to Michael Schumacher during his spell as Ferrari's number two driver.

10) Jody Scheckter, the South African winner of the 1979 title, whose elder brother, Ian, drove for March and Williams among others between 1974 and 1977.

11) Nigel Mansell, who finished second in 1986, 1987 and 1991 before taking the drivers' crown in 1992.

12) Kubica was the first Polish driver to win a Formula One Grand Prix.

13) Vettel incurred a fine for speeding in the pit lane on the way to the track only six seconds after moving off, which remains the fastest recorded race penalty.

14) Monza, home of the Italian Grand Prix, hosted its 63rd race in 2013.

15) Keke Rosberg, though born in Sweden, raced for Finland. His son Nico was born in Wiesbaden, Germany.

16) Giancarlo Fisichella, who won the 2006 Malaysian Grand Prix for Renault.

17) Emmerson Fittipaldi (1974), James Hunt (1976), Niki Lauda (1984), Alain Prost (1985, 1986, 1989), Ayrton Senna (1988, 1990, 1991), Mika Hakkinen (1998, 1999).

18) They are all features of the iconic Monaco street circuit.

19) Schumacher made his debut for Jordan-Ford in the 1991 Belgian Grand Prix. He qualified seventh on the grid but was forced to retire on lap one with a clutch problem.

20) Damon Hill, who won the title driving a Williams Renault in 1996.